A LIFE BEYOND AMAZING

A LIFE BEYOND AMAZING

9 DECISIONS THAT WILL TRANSFORM YOUR LIFE TODAY

DR. DAVID JEREMIAH

W PUBLISHING GROUP

AN IMPRINT OF THOMAS NELSON

thomasnelson.com

© 2017 David P. Jeremiah
Box 3838, San Diego, CA 92163

Published in Nashville, Tennessee, by W Publishing, an imprint of Thomas Nelson. W Publishing and Thomas Nelson are registered trademarks of HarperCollins Christian Publishing, Inc.

Published in association with Yates & Yates, LLP, www.yates2.com.

All Scripture quotations, unless otherwise indicated, are taken from the *New King James Version*. Copyright © 1982 by Thomas Nelson. Used by permission. All rights reserved.

Scripture quotations marked KJV are from the *King James Version*. Public domain.

Scripture quotations marked NIV taken from the *New International Version®*, NIV®. Copyright © 1973, 1978, 1984, 2011 by Biblica, Inc.® Used by permission. All rights reserved worldwide.

Scripture quotations marked NLT are from the *Holy Bible, New Living Translation*. © 1996, 2004, 2007, 2013, 2015 by Tyndale House Foundation. Used by permission of Tyndale House Publishers, Inc., Carol Stream, Illinois 60188. All rights reserved

Edited by William Kruidenier

Thomas Nelson titles may be purchased in bulk for educational, business, fund-raising, or sales promotional use. For information, please e-mail SpecialMarkets@ThomasNelson.com.

ISBN 978-0-310-09117-2

First printing October 2017 / Printed in the United States of America

Contents

How to Use This Guide

The purpose of this study guide is to reinforce Dr. David Jeremiah's dynamic, in-depth teaching and to aid you in applying biblical truth to your daily life. This study guide is designed to be used in conjunction with Dr. Jeremiah's *A Life Beyond Amazing* book and audio series, but it may also be used by itself for personal or group study.

STRUCTURE OF THE LESSONS

Each lesson is based on one of the messages in the *A Life Beyond Amazing* audio series and book and focuses on specific passages in the Bible. Each lesson is composed of the following elements:

- **Outline:** The outline at the beginning of the lesson gives a clear, concise picture of the topic being studied and will provide a helpful framework for you as you listen to Dr. Jeremiah's teaching or read the book.

- **Overview:** The overview summarizes Dr. Jeremiah's teaching on the passage being studied in the lesson. You should refer to the Scripture passages in your own Bible as you study the overview. Unless otherwise indicated, Scripture verses quoted are taken from the *New King James Version*.

- **Application:** This section contains a variety of discussion questions designed to help you dig deeper into the lesson and the Scriptures and to apply the lesson to your daily life. For Bible study groups or Sunday school classes, these questions will provide a springboard for group discussion and interaction.

- **Did You Know?** This section presents a fascinating fact, historical note, or insight that adds a point of interest to the preceding lesson.

PERSONAL STUDY

The lessons in this study guide were created to help you gain fresh insights into God's Word and develop new perspectives on topics you may have previously studied. Each lesson is designed to challenge your thinking and help you grow in your knowledge of Christ. During your study, it is our prayer that you will discover how biblical truth affects every aspect of your life and your relationship with Christ will be strengthened.

When you commit to completing this study guide, try to set apart a time, daily or weekly, to read through the lessons without distraction. Have your Bible nearby when you read the study guide, so you're ready to look up verses if you need to. If you want to use a notebook to write down your thoughts, be sure to have that handy as well. Take your time to think through and answer the questions. If you plan on reading the study guide with a small group, be sure to read ahead and be prepared to take part in the weekly discussions.

GROUP STUDY

The lessons in this study guide are suitable for Sunday school classes, small-group studies, elective Bible studies, or home Bible study groups. Each person in the group should have his or her own study guide.

When possible, the study guide should be used with the corresponding audio series. You may wish to complete the study guide lesson as homework prior to the group meeting and then use the meeting time to listen to Dr. Jeremiah's teaching and discuss the lesson. If you are a group leader, refer to the guide at the back of this book for additional instructions on how to set up and lead your group time.

FOR CONTINUING STUDY

For a complete listing of Dr. Jeremiah's materials for personal and group study, call 1-800-947-1993, go online to www.DavidJeremiah.org, or write to Turning Point, P.O. Box 3838, San Diego, CA 92163.

Dr. Jeremiah's *Turning Point* program is currently heard or viewed around the world on radio, television, and the Internet in English. *Momento Decisivo*, the Spanish translation of Dr. Jeremiah's messages, can be heard on radio in every Spanish speaking country in the world. The television broadcast is also broadcast by satellite throughout the Middle East with Arabic subtitles.

Contact Turning Point for radio and television program times and stations in your area, or visit our website at www.DavidJeremiah.org/stationlocator.

A Life Beyond Amazing

Jesus of Nazareth wasn't the only influential figure who appeared on the Judean scene in the two centuries surrounding His birth. But He is the only one who changed the world because He was the only one from God (Acts 5:33–39).

Why were people drawn to Jesus? Why did they follow Him then, and why do they still follow Him today? For at least three reasons: His miracles, His teachings, and His character. Jesus' miracles and teachings have received ample attention through the years, much more than His character. Ironically, it is His character that Christians have been called to develop. He has not charged His followers with producing miracles or creating teachings of their own. (We have His miracles and His teachings in the Scriptures.) But we have been empowered to display His character.

What was His character like? The people in first-century Judea were not used to a person who lived a life of love, joy, peace, endurance, compassion, generosity, integrity, humility, and self-discipline *day in and day out*. Everyone is loving sometimes, joyful on occasion, and peaceful when in non-stressful circumstances. Said another way, everyone has moments, or days, when they demonstrate the opposite of Jesus' character. The people of that day were not used to someone demonstrating those and other godly traits *all the time*. Jesus' character, as much as His miracles and teachings, caused people to continually ask, "Who is this Man?"

Fast forward to Paul's letter to the Galatians, where he draws a distinction between "normal" people and Spirit-filled people. We know what the character of "normal" people is like (Paul gives some examples in Galatians 5:19–21). But then Paul does what Jesus' biographers didn't do: he gives a list of nine character traits that born-again people can cultivate in their lives, calling them "the fruit of the Spirit" (verses 22–23). Jesus was anointed by, and filled with, the Holy Spirit and manifested these traits in His life—the fruit of the Spirit of God in a human being who was submitted to the Spirit's lordship. And the same can be true in the life of a Christian who is submitted to the leading of the Spirit of God. We can have the character of Jesus Christ. We can manifest the fruit of the Spirit.

Paul later wrote that the ultimate purpose of the Christian's life is to be conformed to the image of Christ (Romans 8:29). As we submit to the empowering presence of the Holy Spirit, we allow Christ to live His life through us: "It is no longer I who live, but Christ lives in me; and the life which I now live in the flesh I live by faith in the Son of God" (Galatians 2:20). How do we know when Christ is living His life fully through us? When our lives show the fruit of the Holy Spirit; when our lives are loving, joyful, peaceful, enduring, compassionate, generous, faithful, humble, and self-disciplined.

When we live a life like that, we will be living a life that is beyond amazing—a life that the world is not used to seeing and a life we cannot experience on our own. It is the purpose of this *A Life Beyond Amazing* study guide to paint a picture of a life that displays the fruit of the Spirit. It is a life yielded to the Holy Spirit so He is free to reveal Christ in us to the world around us.

The world today needs the same thing the first-century world needed—the presence of God in our midst. And when the followers of Christ today manifest the fruit of His Spirit, the world today will be drawn to history's most beyond-amazing life: Jesus Christ.

A Life Beyond Amazing

SELECTED SCRIPTURES

In this lesson we are introduced to the theme of a Christian life beyond amazing: the roadblocks, roadmaps, and results.

Jesus Christ lived an amazing life and attracted followers wherever He went. But the same can't always be said of His followers today, the Church. When we understand that our salvation is more than just a past event, we catch a biblical vision for the amazing life God wants us to experience.

OUTLINE

I. **The Roadblocks to a Life Beyond Amazing**
   A. A Misunderstanding of Salvation
   B. A Misapplication of "Works"
   C. A Mistaken Idea of Spirituality

II. **The Roadmap to a Life Beyond Amazing**

III. **The Result of a Life Beyond Amazing**

OVERVIEW

In a recent book, I asked the question, "Is this the end?" The answer to that question is, "No, but you can see it from here." Meaning, every day we are getting closer to the return of Jesus Christ. That raises another question: "What kind of people do we need to be to live in an increasingly chaotic and unpredictable culture?" In other words, regardless of what is going on around us, what kind of people does God expect us to be?

The answer is in this series of lessons. We need to be the kind of people described in Galatians 5:22–23—people who manifest the fruit of the Holy Spirit: love, joy, peace, longsuffering, kindness, goodness, faithfulness, gentleness, and self-control. That is the kind of person Jesus Christ was. The indwelling Holy Spirit wants to manifest the presence of Christ in and through us as well.

I call such a life "a life beyond amazing"—the abundant life Jesus came to give us (John 10:10). It is an impossible life apart from the Holy Spirit. But it is possible by His power and presence. In this series we will examine each of the nine dimensions of the fruit of the Spirit, one at a time.

The Roadblocks to a Life Beyond Amazing

Are you, or the Christians you know, living a life beyond amazing? If not, what is getting in the way? How can we remove the impediments? I know three obstacles that can stand in our way.

A Misunderstanding of Salvation

First, we mistake the nature of salvation by thinking of it only in the past tense—something that happened "back then." But the Bible views salvation in three "tenses": past, present, and future.

First, we *have been saved*. At a moment in the past we placed our faith in Christ and were saved. Second, we *are being saved* continually and daily delivered from the power of sin. Finally, we *will be saved* for all eternity in God's heavenly kingdom. So our salvation is three-fold: from the *penalty* of sin (past), the *power* of sin (present), and the *presence* of sin (future) (Romans 13:11).

Unfortunately, too many Christians are stuck in the past. They fail to walk in the ongoing blessings and benefits of salvation in the present. They know they were saved *from* something, but they have failed to realize they were also saved *for* something. And what we have been saved *for* is a beyond-amazing life. It's like being adopted into a family and then spending many years coming to realize the benefits and blessings of that family. As author Craig Barnes says, "How long does it take to become a Christian? A moment—and a lifetime!"

Becoming a Christian is not the end of one kind of life, it should be the beginning of another: a life beyond amazing!

A Misapplication of "Works"

The New Testament is clear that we are not saved by our good works; we are saved as a gift of grace (Ephesians 2:8–9; Titus 3:5). But it is also clear that we are "created in Christ Jesus for good works" (Ephesians 2:10; see also Titus 3:8). We are not saved *by* good works but *for* good works. Too many Christians think that because their salvation is a gift, they can be passive about it until they get to heaven. Not true! We are saved unto an active, Christlike life while on earth.

A Mistaken Idea of Spirituality

Some Christian teachers promote an idea of spirituality called "the deeper life." Essentially, they say, "Let go and let God." It means to put our trust completely in God (a good thing) to accomplish everything in us without our involvement (not good). I believe this view downplays the importance of the Christian's responsibility to be active in pursuing the spiritual life; we have to fight the good fight of faith. Yes, God does the work in us, but we actively pursue those things that we know God is working in us to accomplish. Our spirituality is active, not passive. It takes time; it doesn't happen all at once.

Our initial salvation happens in a moment of time, but the working out of our salvation—our conformation to the image of Christ (Romans 8:29)—takes a lifetime.

The Roadmap to a Life Beyond Amazing

Having identified the obstacles that stand in our way to a beyond-amazing life, where do we find the roadmap?

Philippians 2:12–13 is a good place to begin—Paul balances our work and God's work together: "Work out your own salvation . . . for it is God who works in you." Please note that Paul is not saying to work *for* our salvation but to work *out* our salvation—live it out as God does His transforming work in us. It's like a miner who works to *bring to the surface* something God put deep in the earth. God put it there (in us), and we work to reveal His work in us. We work *out* what God has worked *in*. The New Testament holds our work and God's work in perfect balance—and so should we.

Peter agrees: God's "divine power has given to us all things that pertain to life and godliness" (2 Peter 1:3). But we are to add to our faith virtue, knowledge, self-control, perseverance, godliness, brotherly kindness, and love (verses 5–7). We are to give "all diligence" (verse 5) to these things. That sounds active, not passive, to me!

What does that roadmap look like? Paul continues in Philippians 2: we will be found "blameless and harmless" in the midst of a chaotic world (verses 14–16). That's how we shine God's amazing light in a dark world—by maxing out what God has done for us and in us. We are to work out our salvation daily, bringing to light the glory of Christ in us for the world to see.

Paul wrote to Timothy to "reject" the bad things and "exercise" himself toward godliness (1 Timothy 4:7). The origin of the word "exercise" is the Greek word for *gymnasium*. We are to go to the spiritual gym daily to perfect our spirituality. The Holy Spirit doesn't force us to conform to the fruit of the Spirit; He enables us to pursue them by His power. That is the roadmap to a life beyond amazing.

The Result of a Life Beyond Amazing

If we remove the roadblocks and follow the roadmap, what will be the results of the life we will live? I call it character—the bridge between our past and future salvation experiences. The life we now live between those two consists of the godly character we pursue and develop with the help of the Holy Spirit. We are to pursue traits like the fruit of the Holy Spirit and others in an active way, enabled by the Spirit. As our character is transformed, we work out our salvation in the present. But it doesn't happen overnight while we sleep. It happens as we exercise our character so it is conformed to the character of Christ.

Author Pat Goggins has expressed what it means to develop character through self-discipline:

I describe Character as the only thing that goes in the casket with you. It's the only thing that you take with you to the hereafter. Everything else—all the ranches, the farms, the money, the machinery, the good horses, the top cattle—these are all wonderful attributes, but they do not go in the box with you. Character does!

People of strong character are usually people that are very well self-disciplined. They have fortitude, integrity, and ethical strength. These are attributes that will distinguish each one of us from another, and the combination of these qualities is what you call Character.

Character is an attitude that every young person, every middle-age person, every old person should have embedded in their minds. Character is returning extra change at the grocery store. Character is keeping appointments and being on time, honoring your commitments and honoring your word. Character is choosing the harder right instead of the easier wrong. Character is setting priorities that honor God, family, country, and then career.

Character in marriage is working through the tough times rather than throwing in the towel and looking at divorce. Character is being committed to the well-being of your family and friends, associates, and others, even if it is personally costly; and yes, Character is setting a good example.

A married person of Character acts married all the time. A person of Character is self-disciplined and self-controlled. Character implies the courage to stand for what is right, if necessary, all alone to oppose what is wrong and to make the effort to discern the difference. Character is being truthful in all things while being sensitive to the fact that sometimes the truth hurts and need not be spoken. Character is being selfless rather than selfish.

Character in its true form is developed over time and, just like steel, is forged to its greatest strength. The fires of daily living are the fires that hone Character.

Remember, it's the only thing that goes in the casket with you to the hereafter, and believe it or not, it's the only thing that people will remember about you when you're gone.[1]

Our world is crying out for people of character; it doesn't take much for a person of Christlike character to stand out in this world. I want to be that person, and I hope you do as well. I want to live a life beyond amazing!

Every time we involve ourselves in the life of others in this world—family, community, workplace, church—we have the opportunity to display the character of Christ. It may not always be easy; it may require hard work and difficult choices. But that's why the Bible uses such terms like "work out," "exercise," "pursue," and "run the race." When we implement that idea in our spiritual life, the result will be a life that people notice and are attracted to. We don't want them to be attracted to us in our flesh but to Jesus Christ who is revealing His life and character through us.

British theologian N. T. Wright tells a story about a village church whose choir needed help. They tried, but the result was not very good. Then a new choir director came on board and began to work with the choir. He was gentle and encouraging, but firm and skillful. His goal, through practice and leadership, was to take them beyond where they had been, to take them to the point of being what a choir should be. And it worked! Wright visited that church some time later and discovered a choir fully engaged in leading the congregation in worship. He goes on to say that is how God's grace works in our lives. God finds us in not very good shape and gracefully works with us over time to where we are singing in tune with Him more and more. He takes us where we are and leads us to where He knows we can be—and where we know we want to be.

Wright compares the Christian life to that of a musician or singer: "Out of our desire to become better musicians, we begin to *practice* and to *learn the habits* of how to sing. . . . There is the sequence: grace, which meets us where we are but is not content to let us remain where we are, followed by direction and guidance to enable us to acquire the right habits to replace the wrong ones."[2]

You may have joined God's "choir"—been saved—many years ago. Or you may be new to the choir. In either case, it is time to tune up, develop our skills (character), and let the Holy Spirit lead us into the amazing life

Christ died to provide for us. We remove the roadblocks, become familiar with the roadmap, then start working toward the results, with God's help, that Scripture clearly identifies for us.

The greatest illustration of the theme of this lesson is this: almighty God loved us before the foundation of the world (Ephesians 1:4). And that would be enough, would it not? But God didn't leave it at that. He loved us enough to send us His own Son to prove His sacrificial love. He gave us Christ, the incarnation of true humanity, to see what our own potential is. God acted to demonstrate His love to you and to me and wants to lead us to fulfill His loving desires.

Perhaps you are reading this study guide but have never taken the step to receive God's love; you have never been saved. If that is the case, you can never move ahead to the amazing life that God has planned for you. I urge you today to put your faith in Christ, to open your heart to Him. Ask Him to forgive your sins and lead you into the transformation of your life for His glory. Once you take that step and are assured of your salvation in the *past*, you can begin experiencing God's *present* salvation (transformation) and can know without doubt that your *eternal* salvation awaits you in God's kingdom yet to come.

APPLICATION

Personal Questions

1. Describe the type of person you think God wants you to be.

   a. The biblical description of a life beyond amazing is found in Galatians 5:22–23. Describe that life. Why is it an amazing life?

   b. Which of the character traits listed in Galatians 5:22–23 are evident in your life? Which of them do you most need to cultivate?

2. What are the three common roadblocks to a life beyond amazing?

   Which of the three roadblocks is most keeping you from becoming the person God wants you to be?

3. Philippians 2:12–13 is the roadmap to a beyond-amazing life.

   a. What is Paul *not* saying about salvation in these verses?

   b. What *is* Paul saying about salvation in these verses?

   c. Second Peter 1:3 says God has given us His divine power to live this life beyond amazing. According to 2 Peter 1:5–7, how are we to respond to God's gift of divine power?

4. When you remove the roadblocks and follow the roadmap to a life beyond amazing, you will become a person of character.

   a. Describe what it means to be a person of character.

   b. How have people of character influenced your life for your good? How have you influenced others for their good?

5. Living the life that Christ has called you to takes commitment. In His grace, Christ has committed Himself to your spiritual growth. Are you ready to commit your life to Him and to the life He has called you to?

Group Questions
1. Discuss what an amazing life looks like according to the world.

a. How would you define an amazing life?

b. The biblical description of a life beyond amazing is found in Galatians 5:22–23. How does the life described in those verses differ from the world's view of an amazing life?

c. Which of the character traits listed in Galatians 5:22–23 are most needed in our world today? Which are the most difficult to cultivate?

2. Talk about the differences between being saved from the *penalty* of sin, the *power* of sin, and the *presence* of sin.

a. How should this mindset of salvation affect how we live our lives?

b. What is the danger in getting stuck in the past tense of salvation?

3. Read Philippians 2:12–13.

a. How is working *out* your salvation different from working *for* your salvation?

b. What is God's role in salvation? What is ours?

4. Developing our character is the bridge between our past and future salvation experiences. It's an amazing life.

a. What is character?

b. How is character developed?

5. In this lesson, grace is defined as that "which meets us where we are but is not content to let us remain where we are."

   a. How does this definition encourage you?

   b. Is it more difficult for you to meet people where they are or challenge them to an amazing life?

   c. Discuss how your relationships would look if you both accepted others as they are and encouraged them toward a life beyond amazing.

DID YOU KNOW?

When Paul tells Timothy to "exercise [himself] toward godliness" (1 Timothy 4:7), he uses the Greek verb *gumnazo*—to exercise, to train, to discipline. It is easy to see the root of our English word *gymnasium* in the Greek word. The word *gumnazo* literally meant "to exercise naked in the arena," an image of the Greek athlete throwing off all encumbrances to his training regimen—including clothes! The writer to the Hebrews certainly conveyed that idea in a spiritual sense: "Let us lay aside every weight, and the sin which so easily ensnares us, and let us run with endurance the race that is set before us" (Hebrews 12:1).

Notes
1. Pat Goggins, "Character, the One Thing that Goes in the Casket with You," *Western Ag Reporter*, January 7, 2016.
2. N. T. Wright, *After You Believe* (New York: HarperOne, 2011), 63.

A Life of Love

EPHESIANS 5:1–2

*In this lesson we discover what it means to love others
the way God loves us.*

It is ironic that what the world needs more than anything is something the world knows little about. And that is true love—the biblical kind of love. While modern love in the world is "me" centered, biblical love is "others" centered. We are to love others the way Jesus Christ loves us.

OUTLINE

I. The Command to Love

II. The Cultivation of Love

III. The Challenges to Love
  A. Reflect on God's Love for You
  B. Pursue Genuine Love
  C. Pray for Greater Love
  D. Don't Be Afraid to Risk
  E. Practice Love Every Day

OVERVIEW

Nothing is more talked about, sung about, joked about, and written about—and less understood today—than love. Is loving pizza really supposed to be the same as loving God or one's spouse? People like the idea of love, and most people desperately want to be loved (whatever that means to them), but most people don't understand true love at all.

The Bible mentions love hundreds of times, of course; it is the core theme in God's redemptive plan for man: "For God so loved the world . . ." (John 3:16). Love is also the first of the nine dimensions of the fruit of the Spirit mentioned by Paul: "The fruit of the Spirit is love . . ." (Galatians 5:22). Not to mention that God Himself is love (1 John 4:8, 16). When we talk about the kind of people we should be, from a biblical perspective we must begin with love "because the love of God has been poured out in our hearts by the Holy Spirit" (Romans 5:5).

Love is not just a sentiment or a feeling; love is action. It's impossible to read Paul's Love Chapter (1 Corinthians 13) without seeing the actions that are implied. Biblical love is selfless and sacrificial, always doing what is best for others. That is the kind of love the world is missing. Prior to Christ, love in the pagan world was self-centered; but Jesus' love was so different from anything anyone had seen before that it was given a special name. They called it *agape* love.

I don't know where I first read it, but one of the best definitions of *agape* love is this: "*Agape* love is the power that moves us to respond to someone's needs with no expectation in return." We love others without waiting for them to say thank you. We love as a choice; it is predicated by our values and our beliefs, not on our expectation of anything in return. The ultimate illustration of that kind of love is the Cross of Calvary, where Jesus died willingly and sacrificially for us. We were totally unworthy; we often do not respond gratefully; yet Jesus loved us all the same.

In this lesson, we will talk about imitating God's love for us as a template for how we are to love one another: "Imitate God, therefore. . . . Live a life filled with love, following the example of Christ" (Ephesians 5:1–2 NLT). We are commanded to be people of love.

The Command to Love

Love is a command, not a suggestion or an option. This confuses the world because it is used to the idea of "falling" in love—love is something that just "happens." Love is out of our control. But that is not the biblical idea of love. Over and over in the New Testament, we are commanded to love—John 13:34; 15:12, 17; 1 John 3:23; and more. Thirteen of those commands are for us to love one another.

We sometimes think Christ's kind of *agape* love is impossible and we justify failing to love others. But would Christ command us to do something He doesn't give us the power to do? That's why love is a fruit *of the Spirit*. By the Spirit's empowerment, we can love others as Christ loves us (Ephesians 4:32).

The Cultivation of Love

God has deposited His love in us (Romans 5:5), but it is up to us to put that love into action by actually loving others. After Paul's beautiful chapter on love in 1 Corinthians 13, the very next thing he writes is, "Pursue love . . ." (1 Corinthians 14:1). He describes love in chapter 13 and then immediately says, "Now pursue it; put it into action!"

There is a paradox here, isn't there? We are given love as a gift from God that the Spirit manifests as a fruit of His presence, but it is up to us to pursue it! Love is a gift we are given to use, not to put on a shelf and admire.[1] But we know it is not easy; it takes work to love others.

The Challenges to Love

No Christian is exempt from the responsibility to love others with a Christlike love. You may struggle to love, but that doesn't excuse you. We have God's love as an example of how we are to love one another. Here are five ways to become a more loving person.

Reflect on God's Love for You

You probably know John 3:16 by heart, but consider 1 John 3:16: "By this we know love, because He laid down His life for us. And we also ought to lay down our lives for the brethren." And 1 John 4:11–12 carries a similar message. My point is that one of the ways we learn to love others is by considering how much God loved us. We must love others the same way.

The first Medal of Honor awarded for combat in Afghanistan went (posthumously) to Lieutenant Michael Murphy, a Navy SEAL. He and his three team members were surrounded and trapped by more than fifty Taliban fighters. They fought until they ran out of ammunition. To get a clear radio signal to call for help, Lieutenant Murphy exposed himself to enemy fire, being shot twice in the back while calling for help. One of the team survived because his commander gave up his own life in an attempt to get help for the whole team.

That's an example of sacrificial love—laying down one's life for another (John 15:13). That is the love that the modern "me" generation knows little of. We must guard against absorbing the world's definition of love and consider how God loves us. "While we were still sinners, Christ died for us" (Romans 5:8)—that is God's kind of love.

Lieutenant Murphy's men were trapped by the enemy, and he gave his life to save them. Likewise, we were trapped by the power and penalty of sin, and Jesus gave up His life to save us. Medal of Honor love is awesome, but Cross of Calvary love is the ultimate. As we reflect on that love, we will be reminded to love the same way.

Pursue Genuine Love

Second, we need to pursue genuine love. We need to pursue pure love that is "without hypocrisy" (Romans 12:9). When someone says, "How are you?" our automatic answer is often, "Fine." But are we fine? We are in the habit of living lives that are not transparent and honest. If we are going to love with a pure love, we need to love without hypocrisy. Our love and our life need to be sincere.

Pastor Ray Ortlund has pointed out how the beautiful one-another commands in the New Testament *don't* include commands like these: humble one another, pressure one another, corner one another, shame one another, and the like.[2] Instead, the predominant one-another command in the New Testament is to love one another (twelve times). When we begin to love one another with a pure Christlike kind of love, the world will begin to take notice just as Jesus said they would: "By this all will know that you are My disciples, if you have love for one another" (John 13:35). Jesus' love was a pure love and ours must be pure as well.

How will the world know we are followers of Jesus? By our church attendance? Our financial contributions? By the time we spend in prayer? Those are good things and may attract the attention of the world, but Jesus said nothing about them. He said only one thing would tell the world we are His: love. When Christians—individuals and groups—can't get along with one another, the world takes it as a negative message about Jesus. But if we love Jesus' way, the world will take that as a positive message about Him.

Pursue love. Not the world's kind of love, but the genuine love by which God first loved us.

Pray for Greater Love

This next step may seem obvious, but how often do we do it? *Pray for greater love!* If loving others is a challenge in general—or perhaps the challenge is loving a particular individual—then pray and ask God for the grace to love unconditionally and sacrificially.

If the apostle Paul is a role model for us (and he is—1 Corinthians 4:16; 11:1), then we can follow his example as he prayed for others to love well. Writing to the Philippians, he told them of his prayers that their love "may abound still more and more" (Philippians 1:9). He wanted the Philippians to love even more so he prayed that they would. Paul also prayed that the Ephesians would come to know the "width and length and depth and height" of God's love (Ephesians 3:18-19).

If Paul prayed for a greater realization and practice of God's love for first-century Christians, why shouldn't we pray for the same thing for ourselves and others? Even if we didn't have Paul's examples, there are enough admonitions to prayer in the New Testament that love can be easily included. In fact, it probably should be a permanent addition to every believer's prayer list: "Lord, help me to love with a genuine love the way Christ loves me."

God wants us to be loving people; He doesn't mind if we ask Him to help us. And, if you have somebody in your life who is not very loving toward you and others, pray for them that God would give them greater love, too.

Don't Be Afraid to Risk

Number four in this list is a challenge for many of us: Don't be afraid to risk loving others; don't be afraid to obey the commands of Scripture and leave the results to God. Sometimes when we try to love (help) another person, he or she repays us with an ungrateful attitude or action. None of us likes to be hurt. So it's tempting just to withhold our love rather than risk getting wounded. But that is not a reason to withhold love for anyone.

Many people, especially younger people, may declare their love for someone who then leaves them behind. They swear they will never love again; better to not love than to love and get hurt. Those people must heed the words of C. S. Lewis:

> To love at all is to be vulnerable. Love anything, and your heart will certainly be wrung and possibly be broken. If you want to make sure of keeping it intact, you must give your heart to no one, not even to an animal. Wrap it carefully round with hobbies and little luxuries; avoid all entanglements; lock it up safe in the casket or coffin of your selfishness. But in that casket—safe, dark, motionless, airless—it will change. It will not be broken; it will become unbreakable, impenetrable, irredeemable. The alternative to tragedy, or at least to the risk of tragedy, is damnation. The only place outside Heaven where you can be perfectly safe from all the dangers and perturbations of love is Hell.[3]

We must trust God—what we sow we shall reap (Galatians 6:7). If you sow love, you may not reap love immediately. But God always rewards obedience to His Word and will do so if we will step out in faith and love.

Practice Love Every Day

Finally—last but not least—we must practice love every day. We are to "be imitators of God" and "walk in love" (Ephesians 5:1–2).

Walking means taking one step at a time. Walking for a young child means falls and failures. But the more they try, the more they practice, walking becomes second nature. When we love in everything we do (1 Corinthians 16:14), the better we will become at loving in every situation and toward every person.

Learning to love every day doesn't mean one big love project where we show the world how loving we are. Rather, it means loving in the small, daily matters that challenge us and test our commitment to God and His Word—especially in those situations where no one is watching, where no reward is likely, and where we stand a chance of being hurt for our efforts.

Sometimes we're tempted to make a show of our love, like putting a $1,000 check in the offering on Sunday. Craig Larson has a better idea:

[God] sends us to the bank and has us cash in the $1,000 for quarters. We go through life putting out 25 cents here and 50 cents there. Listen to the neighbor kid's troubles instead of saying, "Get lost." Go to a committee meeting. Give a cup of water to a shaky old man in a nursing home. Usually giving our life to Christ isn't glorious. It's done in all those little acts of love, 25 cents at a time.[4]

So—yield to the command to love, cultivate love, and implement the challenges to become a more loving person. That is the way we learn to love others as God loves us.

APPLICATION

Personal Questions

1. People use the word *love* in many different ways. What does the word mean to you?

   a. What is *agape* love?

   b. What is the difference between our world's definition of love and God's *agape* love? List characteristics of each.

2. Biblical love is not just a feeling; it's an action. Read 1 Corinthians 13:1–13 and do the following:

   a. List the areas where you display God's love most often and offer a reason why this is so in your life.

      Trait: Reason:

      Trait: Reason:

      Trait: Reason:

   b. List the areas where you feel you could more clearly demonstrate God's love to others and make an action plan on how you will begin that process.

      Trait: Reason:

      Trait: Reason:

      Trait: Reason:

3. In this lesson, you discovered five ways to become a more loving person. List them and consider how you can practice them in your life.

   a.

   b.

   c.

   d.

   e.

Group Questions

1. People use the word *love* in many different ways. Discuss as a group what the word means to each of you.

   a. Talk about God's love. What is *agape* love?

   b. What is the difference between God's *agape* love and our world's definition of love?

2. Biblical love is not just a feeling; it's an action. Read 1 Corinthians 13:1–13 and discuss what true love looks like in everyday life.

3. Love is a command, not a suggestion or an option. Find three verses that command us to love and read them aloud.

   a. Discuss why Jesus can command us to love one another.

   b. Share some ideas of how your group can showcase God's love to each other and to those in your community.

4. In this lesson, we've discovered five ways to become a more loving person. List them and consider how you can encourage each other to practice them on a day-to-day basis.

   a.

   b.

   c.

   d.

e.

f.

5. The apostle Paul prayed that our love would "abound still more and more" (Philippians 1:9). Take a few moments to pray for each other, asking God to make us people who know God's love more deeply and love others more fully.

DID YOU KNOW?

Agape was not the only first-century Greek word for love. *Agape* existed before the New Testament but was used very rarely. It was the New Testament writers who provided its unique status as the defining word for God's active love for man. Another Greek word, *eros*, is not found in the New Testament. It referred to a sensual, erotic kind of attraction and activity. Another Greek word, *philanthropia* (and the verb *phileo*), is used extensively in the New Testament. It is the word for "tender affection" (see Acts 28:2—"unusual kindness"). (Note that Philadelphia, Pennsylvania, is called "the city of brotherly love" based on the Greek *phileo* and *adelphos*—"love" and "brother.")

Notes

1. Philip D. Kenneson, *Life on the Vine: Cultivating the Fruit of the Spirit* (Downers Grove, IL: InterVarsity Press, 1999), 42.
2. Ray Ortlund, "'One Anothers' I Can't Find in the New Testament," The Gospel Coalition, March 30, 2017, https://blogs.thegospelcoalition.org/rayortlund/2017/03/30/one-anothers-i-cant-find-in-the-new-testament-2/.
3. C. S. Lewis, *The Four Loves* (New York: Harcourt Brace & Company, 1988), 121.
4. Craig Brian Larson, *750 Engaging Illustrations for Preachers, Teachers, and Writers* (Grand Rapids, MI: Baker Books, 2007), 472.

A Life of Joy

SELECTED SCRIPTURES

*In this lesson we discover the source and the secret to
continual joy in Christ.*

From the world's perspective, joy and happiness in life are correlated with possessions and prestige. From the Bible's perspective, joy is a result of living a life submitted to the lordship of Christ and the leading of the Spirit. Joy is a gift of God manifested in us as the fruit of the Spirit.

OUTLINE

I. The Source of Joy in Your Life
   A. The Center of This Joy—"My Joy"
   B. The Characteristic of This Joy—"Your Joy May Be Full"
   C. The Continuity of This Joy—"Remain in You"

II. The Secret of Joy in Your Life
   A. Surrender Your Life to Jesus Christ
   B. Submit Yourself Totally to the Spirit of God
   C. Study the Word of God
   D. Share Your Life with Others

OVERVIEW

Polls consistently show America ranks below many other nations when it comes to happiness. For all our advantages, resources, and opportunities, only about thirty-five percent of Americans say they are very happy. Millions are depressed or anxious, and suicide levels have been rising for decades. Another survey showed that some of the ten richest nations in the world had the highest levels of depression. It could be said that America has developed "a strange melancholy in the midst of abundance"—the words of a French demographer.[1]

We, as a nation and as individuals, clearly need to adjust our thinking about what constitutes true happiness and joy. We can begin by remembering that God Himself experiences joy: "So shall your God rejoice over you" (Isaiah 62:5). And Isaiah 65:19 quotes God, saying, "I will rejoice in Jerusalem, and joy in My people." Zephaniah the prophet said to Israel, "The LORD your God . . . will rejoice over you" (Zephaniah 3:17).

We, being in God's image, only experience joy because God does. And God wants us to experience joy as He does. Jesus declared as much (John 15:11; 17:13), as did the apostle Paul: "Rejoice in the Lord" (Philippians 4:4). We are commanded to find joy in the context of our relationship with Christ.

The New Testament cites many examples of people who found joy after coming in contact with Christ or His apostles: a crippled woman in Luke 13:13; a leper in Luke 17:15; a paralytic in Acts 3:8. Jesus attended the joyful celebration of a wedding in Cana and gladly provided more wine for the feast when the hosts ran out (John 2:1–11). Joy is part of the nature of the kingdom of God. Jesus came to introduce the kingdom of God and its values, joy being one of them. We shouldn't be surprised to find joy just behind love in the list of the fruit of the Spirit (Galatians 5:22). God wants us to be joyful! "Rejoice always," Paul wrote in 1 Thessalonians 5:16.

Did you know there was joy in heaven the day you became a Christian (Luke 15:10)? And the Bible says there should be joy on earth, even in times of difficulty. Jesus said to "rejoice in that day and leap for joy! For indeed your reward is great in heaven" (Luke 6:23). Peter says we should consider ourselves blessed when we are persecuted for following Christ (1 Peter 4:14). (And the word *blessed* can be translated as "happy.") Paul says we "glory in tribulations" (Romans 5:3), and James famously wrote to "count it all joy" when we have trials in life (James 1:2). Paul commends the Thessalonians for receiving God's Word "with joy of the Holy Spirit" in the midst of persecution (1 Thessalonians 1:6). The early apostles in Jerusalem rejoiced when persecuted for Christ's sake (Acts 5:41).

Maybe the best-known story is that of Paul and Silas in jail in Philippi, having just suffered a terrible beating. Acts 16 records how, at midnight, they were in jail "praying and singing hymns to God" (verse 25). When you can find joy with a bloody back leaning against the cold stone wall of a Roman jail, you have the real thing. Paul even anticipated finishing his life, his "race," with joy (Acts 20:24).

Can you say that? Do you experience the fruit of joy in your life? Do you find joy in every aspect of the life God has provided in Christ and the hope of eternity with Him? We should agree with G. K. Chesterton, who wrote, "Joy . . . is the gigantic secret of the Christian."[2] True joy is found nowhere but in Christ.

The Source of Joy in Your Life

Jesus Christ is the source of our joy. He told His disciples, "These things I have spoken to you, that My joy may remain in you, and that your joy may be full" (John 15:11). Let us look at three aspects of that verse.

The Center of This Joy—"My Joy"

Jesus wants us to be full of *His* joy—Peter called it "joy inexpressible" (1 Peter 1:8). That is the joy of Christ in us. Paul says we are strengthened by God "for all patience and longsuffering with joy" (Colossians 1:11). Our joy isn't dependent on us or our circumstances; it is dependent on Christ in us.

The Characteristic of This Joy—"Your Joy May Be Full"

The word *full* in John 15:11 can also be translated as "complete." Joy is rather abstract, so how do we know we are full of joy? When we understand that our joy in Christ is complete, it is lacking nothing, it is sufficient for every situation in life. Peter makes the point that, even though we've never seen Jesus, we still have complete joy in Him (1 Peter 1:8).

In England, when the monarch is in residence at Buckingham Palace, the monarch's flag is flown from the flagpole. That was the image borrowed by an English headmaster when talking to his students about Christian joy: "Joy is the flag that is flown from the castle of your heart when the King is in residence." And for the Christian, the King is always in residence, isn't He? So our joy can always be full.

The Continuity of This Joy—"Remain in You"

Jesus also said He wanted His joy to remain in us. That means, since our joy is from Jesus, and Jesus is always with us, our joy should never leave us either. Our joy should "remain" in us. It is so easy for our joy to be fleeting; it is easy to allow circumstances to determine our joy. We are used to things not lasting in this life and we think joy won't last either.

On the night before Jesus went to the cross and the disciples were downcast, He told them He would see them again and they would rejoice: "And your joy no one will take from you" (John 16:22). We should always have joy. If our joy is always in Jesus and not in the world, it will always remain with us.

The Secret of Joy in Your Life

Let us turn now to the practical side of this fruit of the Spirit. God gives joy in Christ as a gift, but how do we appropriate it and keep it?

Surrender Your Life to Jesus Christ

If true joy is to be found in Christ, you have to know Christ; Christ has to be Lord and Savior of your life. Knowing Christ is where joy begins—when we realize we have been relieved of all the burden of sin and shame we have carried for so long. Jesus empties our heart and soul of all that baggage so we can be filled with His joy. As Paul wrote, "Old things have passed away; behold, all things have become new" (2 Corinthians 5:17). And one of those new "things" is the joy of the Lord. But we have to be made new—be born again in Christ—for that to be true.

Submit Yourself Totally to the Spirit of God

It happened to David and it could happen to us—losing the *joy* of our salvation (Psalm 51:12). It is possible to be saved but not experience the joy of that salvation. Everyone goes through difficult times in life like David did. If we are not careful, we could get caught in a downward spiral of emotional and spiritual weakness that overcomes the joy that is our inheritance in Christ.

To avoid even considering that downward spiral, we have to stay totally submitted to the Spirit of God. If we are filled with the Spirit (Ephesians 5:18), we will manifest the fruit of the Spirit that is joy. Submission to the Spirit is submission to Christ as Lord. If He, as Lord, allows us to experience difficulty in life, that doesn't mean we forfeit our joy. Total submission to Christ means being filled with the Spirit, which means manifesting the fruit of joy.

There was a time in my life as a very young Christian that I didn't want to submit my life wholly to Christ because I feared He would send me to Africa as a missionary. I know better now—that it is better to be in the will of God in Africa than out of the will of God somewhere else. If Christ is Lord, it means trusting Him and His every direction for our life.

We are faced with crossroads in our life all the time—go God's way or our way? We should settle that question once and for all so we don't reevaluate it every time. Every time we stop to decide afresh if we will submit to God's leading, we are deciding whether to forfeit the fruit of the Spirit in our life—joy included.

As a young man, I thought I wanted to be involved in Christian broadcasting; then God called me to preach. I temporarily gave up the joy of broadcasting to go to seminary, never knowing God would restore and multiply that joy by being involved as a preacher in broadcasting far beyond anything I could ever have imagined. When we are totally submitted to God and the Spirit's leading, we can trust Him instead of leaning on our own understanding (Proverbs 3:5–6).

Study the Word of God

The Bible is our instruction manual on joy. It tells us the source of joy, how it is possible to always have joy, and what can take away our joy if we let it. Without continual reference to the truths of God's Word, it is easy to forget the principles and practice of joy.

The *New King James* translation of the Bible contains more than 400 references to joy, joyful, joyfully, joyous, rejoice, and rejoicing. All we need to do is consistently read God's Word and we will bump into instructions, examples, principles, and truths about joy in the Christian life. You might develop your own system for marking these occurrences of joy in Scripture—use a certain color pen or highlighter to mark them. Then, whenever your joy is being tested, it will be easy to find passages that can encourage you. You will have your own collection of verses, truths, and examples of joy from a divine perspective.

God gave us Scriptures "for doctrine, for reproof, for correction, for instruction in righteousness" (2 Timothy 3:16)—and that includes in the area of joy.

Share Your Life with Others

Finally, joy is one of those things that increases as we give it away; it multiplies as we invest it in others' lives; we reap joy as we sow joy in relationships (Galatians 6:7). It was never God's design or intent for us to be joyful in isolation from others. All the fruit of the Spirit, like the gifts of the Spirit, are given for the strengthening of the Body of Christ. If all Christians were continually manifesting the fruit of the Spirit, think what the Church would be like: loving, joyful, peaceful, patient, kind, good, gentle, faithful, and self-controlled. In this case we're talking about sharing joy—but it applies as well to all the fruit of the Spirit.

The British commentator William Barclay wrote, "The Christian is the man of joy, the laughing cavalier of Christ. A gloomy Christian is a contradiction in terms, and nothing in all religious history has done Christianity more harm than its connection with black clothes and long faces."[3] Our churches should be congregations of joyful people, not collections of somber souls who don't think it's appropriate for godly people to enjoy themselves or the Lord. It's one of the reasons we enjoy up-tempo music in my own church—that kind of music stirs the soul and causes us to feel happy when we hear it. It's a small thing—but every little bit of sharing of joy helps us and helps others. Joy is contagious! The more joyful people we are around—and the more joyful we are—the more joy will spread.

In his autobiography, *Just As I Am*, Billy Graham recalls visiting the home of one of the wealthiest men in the world on a Caribbean island. The man had every comfort and convenience that money could buy, yet he confessed to being "miserable as hell." The Grahams prayed with the man and tried to point him to Christ, who alone could give him the meaning in life he lacked. Later, back in their small bungalow, the pastor of a local church came to visit them. He was full of joy and enthusiasm for Christ and said, "I don't have two [dollars] to my name, but I am the happiest man on this island."[4]

Billy and Ruth Graham talked about which of the two men was the happiest—it was obvious. It is possible to live a wealthy, lonely life without joy. It is also possible to live in fellowship with other joyful people and be full of joy personally. One is the world's solution and the other is the Bible's. God wants us to be part of a community of joy in our local church.

Have you surrendered your life to Jesus Christ and to the Spirit of God? Are you consistently reading God's Word and sharing life with others? If you are, then God's joy should be yours.

APPLICATION

Personal Questions

1. Polls consistently show America ranks below many other nations when it comes to happiness. Why do you think this is so? List three reasons.

2. In this lesson, you discovered that God is a God of joy. When you think of God, do you think of Him as joyful? Why or why not?

   a. What do you think brings God joy?

   b. What does Isaiah 62:5 and Zephaniah 3:17 say brings God joy?

3. Write out three verses that prove that God wants you to be joyful.

a. Do you think joy is a choice?

b. In what ways can you practice choosing joy?

4. John 15:11 was a key verse in this lesson. Look up this verse in your Bible and answer the following questions:

a. Who is the center of Christian joy?

b. What is the characteristic of Christian joy?

c. What is the continuity of Christian joy?

5. List the four strategies to becoming a more joyful person. Choose one and brainstorm ways you can practice it each day this week.

Group Questions

1. Why do you think so many people are searching for joy? Have someone in your group describe a time when he or she experienced great joy.

2. In this lesson, we've discovered that God is a God of joy. When you think of God, do you think of Him as joyful? Discuss why or why not.

3. Find three verses that prove that God wants you to be joyful. Read them aloud. As a group, discuss the following questions:

    a. Do you think joy is a choice? Why or why not?

    b. In what ways can you practice choosing joy?

4. According to John 15:11, who is the source of true joy?

    a. Describe the kind of joy Jesus mentioned in this verse.

    b. According to this verse, what is the goal of Jesus' teaching?

    c. Do you experience joy when reading God's Word? Why or why not?

5. Discuss the four strategies to becoming a more joyful person.

    What are some ways you can encourage each other to practice these strategies?

6. Joy is one of those things that increases as we give it away; it multiplies as we invest it in others' lives. Take a few minutes to discuss how you can sow seeds of joy into your relationships.

DID YOU KNOW?

In a very general sense, joy in the Old Testament was a corporate experience, whereas joy in the New Testament is an individual experience. Within Israel, joy was expressed through harvest and sacrificial feasts, celebrations of victory in battle, achievements of prosperity, and windfalls. That is, joy was generally circumstantial. In the New Testament, via the indwelling of the Holy Spirit, a new dimension of joy was realized: joy not dependent on circumstances; joy in the midst of suffering; joy at all times. Joy is part of the New Testament reality of being in Christ and Christ being in us by the Spirit. Because that is a constant reality, it overrides the effect of circumstances on joy. Good or bad harvests, defeat or victory—we can have joy.

Notes

1. J. P. Moreland and Klaus Issler, *The Lost Virtue of Happiness* (Colorado Springs, CO: NavPress, 2006), 14–15.
2. G. K. Chesterton, *Orthodoxy* (New York: John Lane Company, 1908), 298.
3. William Barclay, *Growing in Christian Faith* (Louisville, KY: Westminster John Knox Press, 2000), 13.
4. Billy Graham, *Just As I Am* (San Francisco: HarperCollins, 1997), 697.

A Life of Peace

In this lesson we discover what peace is and how to grow in our experience of God's peace.

The Bible presents peace in three dimensions: peace *with* God, peace *from* God, and the peace *of* God. Understanding how peace comes from God to us gives us a biblical path to follow.

OUTLINE

I. Describing Peace
  A. We Can Have Peace *with* God
  B. We Can Have Peace *from* God
  C. We Can Have the Peace *of* God

II. Developing Peace
  A. Peace and the Spirit of God
  B. Peace and the Son of God
  C. Peace and the Word of God
  D. Peace and Prayer

OVERVIEW

"The world is becoming a more dangerous place. . . . The worsening conflict in the Middle East, the lack of a solution to the refugee crisis and an increase in deaths from major terrorist incidents have all contributed to the world being less peaceful."[1] This is not just my opinion; it is the opinion of knowledgeable people the world over. And with danger, chaos, and unpredictability comes fear. We have never lived in a time when the spiritual fruit of peace was more in need for those who face fears daily.

God created a peaceful world and will restore the world to peace in the future. In the interim, He sent His Son, the Prince of Peace (Isaiah 9:6), to show us how to have peace in the midst of turmoil. Someday the nations will not lift arms against one another nor "learn war anymore" (Isaiah 2:4). But until the day comes, we need to know something about God's peace. That is one of the reasons Jesus came to earth—to introduce the kingdom of God in the midst of the kingdom of this world. Through Him we can have "the peace of God, which surpasses all understanding" (Philippians 4:7).

The night Jesus was born, the angels of heaven announced, "Peace, goodwill toward men!" (Luke 2:14). He is the One who can bring deep peace and satisfaction to our lives. We long for international peace among nations, of course. But as we wait for the day, we can have personal peace of our own.

Describing Peace

Peace is found in God Himself. Biblical peace is peace *with*, *from*, and *of* God.

We Can Have Peace with God

Peace with God is the beginning point of man's search for peace. It means you and I are at peace with God instead of in a state of enmity with God. And through Christ, "having been justified by faith, we have peace with God" (Romans 5:1). This refers to the end of hostility, not tranquility of mind. We were enemies of God (Romans 5:10); our sins once came between us and God (Isaiah 59:2). But now, having been reconciled to God through Christ (Romans 5:10) we are at peace *with* God.

Commenting on this peace with God, the late Ray Stedman writes, "Our hearts are at peace! . . . Calmness, courage! To use a modern term, and, I think, the most accurate, we have good 'morale.' Our morale is high. We are ready for anything. No ground can be too rough for Christ—and we have Christ. Therefore, we have good morale."[2]

As I look around, I see lots of people whose spiritual morale is low. They have lost their peace; they're worried, discouraged, confused. We often look like people who have forgotten that the Prince of Peace is our Lord and Savior and Friend. But think about it: If we have peace with God, how could anything else be a source of trouble or fear for us? Peace with God is the basis and reason we can have personal peace of mind and heart.

If you want to live a life of peace, you must begin by asking, "Do I have peace with God?" If you don't, you must settle that issue first. If you do, you are ready to receive peace *from* God.

We Can Have Peace from God

Jesus said, "Peace I leave with you, My peace I give to you. . . . Let not your heart be troubled, neither let it be afraid" (John 14:27). Jesus spoke those words just hours before His violent, painful execution. He told the disciples that peace was possible even at the worst moments. Peace in comfortable times is easy; it is when life is hard that we need peace from God. Jesus reiterated the same message in His first post-resurrection appearance to the disciples: "Peace be with you" (John 20:19).

It was His death on the cross that made peace *with* God possible, which makes peace *from* God possible. And peace *from* God results in us enjoying the peace *of* God.

We Can Have the Peace of God

The best commentary on the peace *of* God is Philippians 4:6–7: "Be anxious for nothing, but in everything by prayer and supplication, with thanksgiving, let your requests be made known to God; and the peace of God, which surpasses all understanding, will guard your hearts and minds through Christ Jesus."

Paul wrote those words while a prisoner in Rome. That is the peace of God—entrusting anxieties and worries to God and letting God's peace guard our heart and mind. We can "lie down in peace, and sleep" because we trust in God (Psalm 4:8). You'll never need to take a sleeping pill when you enjoy the peace of God. You can have the most chaotic, unravelling day imaginable and still sleep in peace at night because you trust God.

Paul wrote that the peace of God is like a soldier, a sentry, that stands watch over our heart and mind after we have committed everything to God in prayer. Peace holds up a shield and fends off all attacks of worry, doubt, fear, and anxiety. Imagine a mighty angel of God standing guard over your heart and mind all day and all night.

Don't try to figure out how this works; Paul says that "the peace of God . . . surpasses all understanding"—and that includes yours and mine! Part of the answer lies in Philippians 4:9: "The God of peace will be with you." So, in verse 7, we are promised that the peace of God will guard us; and in verse 9, we are promised that the God of peace will be with us. In the final analysis, we are protected from the world's fears and anxieties.

Developing Peace

There are four main highways upon which the peace of God travels: the Spirit of God, the Son of God, the Word of God, and prayer.

Peace and the Spirit of God

The connection between the Spirit of God and the peace of God is crucial to understand. In John 16:7, Jesus told His disciples that it was good that He was going away (to heaven, after His resurrection). Why? Because only in His absence would the Holy Spirit be given to the disciples (the Church) to give them power to carry out Jesus' command to make disciples in all nations (Matthew 28:19–20). Not to mention that millions of Christians with Christ dwelling in them through the Spirit would result in far greater ministry than Christ could do alone while on earth.

He had promised them peace (John 14:27; 16:33). But that peace would only be theirs after the Spirit filled them and began to manifest the life of Christ in them—what Paul called the fruit of the Spirit (Galatians 5:22–23). So it was the return of Christ to heaven, and the gift of the Holy Spirit, that allows us to have the peace that Christ promised His disciples they could have (along with love, joy, longsuffering, and the rest of the fruit of the Spirit).

The Holy Spirit of God is the one who reproduces the peace of God in our life. It is fundamentally important that we live a Spirit-filled life (Ephesians 5:18), allowing the Spirit to guide us and fill us with the life of Christ. If we desire peace in our life, it will only be there as the Spirit manifests it in and through us. How do we know if we are filled with the Spirit? If we are manifesting the fruit of the Spirit. And when you get to one of those crossroads in life where you are tempted to choose your direction and not God's—you choose God's; you choose peace over worry and fear.

Peace and the Son of God

Jesus told His disciples not to let their hearts be troubled, that His legacy and deposit for them was peace (John 14:1, 27). He told them that in the world they would have tribulation: "But be of good cheer, I have overcome the world" (John 16:33).

Students of history know that Winston Churchill was the leader who rallied Great Britain against the German attacks on their country in 1940. His voice would come over the radio, encouraging the citizens and building their morale. Ray Stedman sees an analogy between Churchill and Christ: "That is what Jesus Christ has done for us. He comes to us in the midst of the struggle when the battle is almost unbearable and the circumstances look impossible and he speaks peace to us and he gives us the encouragement that we need for our morale to go up and then we can go back into the battle and be victorious."[3]

In his book *The Path of Peace*, Henri Nouwen writes, "Keep your eyes on the prince of peace, the one who doesn't cling to his divine power; the one who refuses to turn stones into bread, jump from great heights, and rule with great power; the one who touches the lame, the crippled, and the blind; the one who speaks words of forgiveness and encouragement. . . . Keep your eyes on him who becomes poor with the poor, weak with the weak. He is the source of all peace."[4]

If God gives peace, who can make trouble (Job 34:29)? And if the Lord of peace Himself gives us peace "always in every way" (2 Thessalonians 3:16), what worry should we have? Remember this: no Christ, no peace; know Christ, know peace.

Peace and the Word of God

The longest psalm in the book of Psalms—and the longest chapter in the Bible—is Psalm 119, with 176 verses. And with the exception of one or two verses, the entire psalm is about the Word of God: laws, statutes, principles, commandments, and more. Psalm 119 explains all the benefits of knowing and applying the Word of God in our life. And one of those benefits is peace.

"Great peace have those who love Your law, and nothing causes them to stumble" (Psalm 119:165). Indirectly, the New Testament epistles convey the same truth; in the *New International Version*, seventeen of the twenty-seven New Testament books begin with the phrase "grace and peace." (Always "grace and peace" in that order; you can't experience peace without knowing God's grace.) So the Word of God in the New Testament is accompanied by a prayerful greeting for peace. And we can receive those writings today just as they were received by the original recipients.

As Christians, we are attentive to what God says in His Word. But consider these words of the psalmist: "I will hear what God the LORD will speak, for He will speak peace to His people and to His saints" (Psalm 85:8). Do you receive peace when God the Lord speaks to you through His Word? Whatever the sovereign God says provides a reason for us to be at peace because He is in control. Whatever question I have for God, His answer—whatever it is—is a reason for me to enjoy peace.

This is another opportunity to encourage you to memorize the Word of God. When you are in need of peace, the Holy Spirit can call to mind truths from God's Word to remind you to trust Him and thus enjoy His peace. It is easy to get distracted by circumstances. Having God's Word memorized focuses our thoughts on what can see us through.

Peace and Prayer

I have already touched on this passage of Scripture in this lesson, but it is so central to peace—and to peace via prayer—that it deserves another look: Philippians 4:6–7. Paul tells us to "be anxious for nothing," and anxious means worried. The *King James Version* says, "Be careful for nothing"—literally, "Don't be full of care." Not care as in "concern" and "attentiveness," but care in terms of worry that bad things are happening.

I see three circles when I think about this verse. There's the "Worry Circle," in which there should be nothing! Then there's the "Prayer

Circle," in which there should be everything, since Paul says to pray about everything. Finally, the "Thanksgiving Circle" contains anything God does in answer to your prayers; any way in which God gives you "the peace of God, which . . . will guard your hearts and minds through Christ Jesus" (verse 7).

I recall once being in the Chicago airport, waiting for a flight to return home, when they announced all flights were grounded for at least two hours. When I inquired as to the reason, I was shown a computer screen displaying weather radar. Right over Chicago was a huge red cell of storm clouds. So I got a cup of coffee, sat down, opened my computer, and began waiting out the storm. It lashed ferociously against the tall plate glass windows of the terminal, yet I was dry, warm, safe, and comfortable sitting in the airport. I was at peace while right in the middle of a terrible storm.

During the storm, I remembered Psalm 61:1–4:

Hear my cry, O God . . .
When my heart is overwhelmed;
Lead me to the rock that is higher than I . . .
I will abide in Your tabernacle forever;
I will trust in the shelter of Your wings.

That's what it means to know God's peace in times of trouble. The Spirit, the Son, the Word, and prayer—four reasons never to be without the peace of God.

APPLICATION

Personal Questions

1. What does the word *peace* mean to you?

In what areas of your life are you experiencing peace? In what areas are you experiencing turmoil?

2. Peace *with* God is the beginning point of our search for peace.

   a. Define peace *with* God.

   b. What do Romans 5:1 and Romans 5:6–8 say about this peace *with* God?

   c. Have you made peace with God as is mentioned in these verses?

3. Read John 14:27. Jesus spoke those words about peace *from* God just hours before His painful execution, proving we can have peace at the worst moments.

   a. Can you think of a time in which you felt overwhelmed by adversity and you found God's peace amid the storms of life?

   b. How can that encourage you when you face hardships in the future?

4. The best commentary on the peace *of* God is Philippians 4:6–7.

   a. What was going on in Paul's life when he wrote these words?

   b. Instead of being anxious, what does the apostle Paul tell you to do in verse 6?

c. In the space provided, write down the promise of verse 7.

d. Write down a list of prayer requests that have been causing you anxiety, and then give them to the Lord.

5. Describe the four main highways on which the peace of God travels.

Group Questions

1. Does the current state of the world give you feelings of restlessness? Do you find yourself craving peace?

2. Discuss some ways the word *peace* is used in our world today.

   a. How does Ray Stedman define peace *with* God?

   b. According to Romans 5:1 and Romans 5:6–8, how can we have peace *with* God?

3. The best commentary on the peace *of* God is Philippians 4:6–7. Read those verses aloud and discuss the following questions.

   a. What was going on in Paul's life when he wrote these words?

   b. Instead of being anxious, what does the apostle Paul tell us to do in verse 6?

   c. What is the promise of verse 7?

d. Take a minute to pray for the worries and anxieties of the people in your group.

4. What are the four main highways upon which the peace of God travels? Discuss each one.

5. Read Psalm 61:1–4. How can your group encourage each other in times of hardship to rely on God's peace?

DID YOU KNOW?

The Jewish (Old Testament) and Greek (New Testament) ideas of peace were different. The Greek idea of peace (*eirene*) refers to the absence of conflict nationally or personally. But the Hebrew idea of peace (*shalom*) was much broader and richer in meaning. The basic meaning of *shalom* was to be whole or safe or prosperous, which would include the absence of hostility or conflict. *Shalom* was the condition of everything being right with the world—again, nationally or individually. Given the choice, more people would prefer *shalom* to the less-nuanced *eirene*. When Isaiah foresaw the coming of the Messiah, he called Him *Sar Shalom*—Prince of Peace (Isaiah 9:6).

Notes

1. Adam Withnall, "Global Peace Index 2016," *Independent*, June 8, 2016, http://www.independent.co.uk/news/world/politics/global-peace-index-2016-there-are -now-only-10-countries-in-the-world-that-are-not-at-war-a7069816.html
2. Ray Stedman, "Defense Against Defeat, Part 1," *Authentic Christianity*, accessed May 22, 2017, https://www.raystedman.org/new-testament/ephesians/defense-against-defeat-part-1.
3. Ray Stedman, *Spiritual Warfare* (Waco, TX: Word Books, 1985), 77–78.
4. Henri Nouwen, *The Path of Peace* (New York: Crossroad, 1995), 78.

LESSON 5

A Life of Endurance

SELECTED SCRIPTURES

In this lesson we discover six ways to build up the power of our spiritual endurance.

Trainers draw a distinction between strength and endurance and how to build both. Strength is needed occasionally in life; endurance is needed every day. Whether we are opposed by spiritual persecution or just the challenges of life, we need endurance—the power to persevere to the end.

OUTLINE

I. Embrace Your Adversity

II. Surround Yourself with Champions

III. Find Your Passion and Pursue It

IV. Get Rid of What's Holding You Back

V. Don't Even Think About Quitting

VI. Stay Focused on the Goal

OVERVIEW

The trainer who helps me work out on a regular basis is a committed Christian. He gave me a tip about weightlifting that I believe is very applicable to the Christian life: heavy weights, lifted with fewer repetitions, build greater strength; lighter weights, lifted with more repetitions, build greater endurance.

When it comes to life, most of us can lift a heavy weight now and again. When a major problem appears, we can deal with it. But when it comes to endurance—doing lots of repetitions with the smaller problems we confront every day, week, and month—we are not as well trained. In other words, when it comes to comparing spiritual strength and endurance, we are in greater need of endurance.

Hebrews 10:36 says it well: "For you have need of endurance, so that after you have done the will of God, you may receive the promise." We need endurance because the Christian life, as someone said to me, is so *daily*. We are always on; we must be ready at all times to be faithful and obedient. All of us are wrestling with issues all the time. As were the people Peter wrote to, telling them not to be surprised at the "fiery trial" they were going through (1 Peter 4:12). Or, as one of Job's friends put it, "Yet man is born to trouble, as the sparks fly upward" (Job 5:7). Some troubles are because we belong to Christ; others are simply because we live in a fallen world. But they both demand the same Christlike response. They both demand endurance.

The writer of Hebrews was writing to people who had been Christians for a while; they weren't new believers. And one of the central themes was endurance. Why? Because it appears they had endured some persecution but now had become spiritually relaxed, maybe complacent, and had let down their spiritual guard. Then persecution began again, and there was talk among them of capitulating, of abandoning their commitment to the faith—returning to Judaism.

The writer reminds them in Hebrews 10:32–34 of what they had already endured. It was then that he told them not to "cast away [their] confidence. . . . For you have need of endurance" (verses 35–36). That is a central theme of Hebrews. After using the earlier chapters to explain why Christ had fulfilled the Jewish structures they had left behind, the writer exhorts them not to go back; he exhorts them to endure the trials they were experiencing.

We need that same message. You may not think you are in danger of going back, but we don't know what the future holds. We need endurance every day to overcome life's daily trials. In this lesson we will discover six ways to strengthen our endurance.

Embrace Your Adversity

God teaches us endurance by allowing us to experience adversity. Is going to the gym painful? Is lifting weights a form of adversity? Yes, and yes. But the result of pain and adversity is strength to endure. If Jesus Christ, God's own Son, had to learn obedience through suffering, why shouldn't we (Hebrews 5:8)?

You are probably familiar with James 1:2-4, where we are told to count our trials as a kind of joy. The joy is in knowing that we will gain patience and maturity from those trials. The apostle Paul makes the same point in Romans 5:3-4, where we learn that "tribulation produces perseverance." We cannot learn to endure without being put in situations that demand endurance!

Most people know who Katie Ledecky is—the American Olympic swimmer who entered the world stage when she won a gold medal in the London Olympic Games in 2012 *at age fifteen*. She won four more golds at the Rio Games in 2016. She doesn't just win her races; she wins by amazing margins. As all great athletes do, she trains relentlessly. She embraces the pain it takes to rise to an Olympic level. She has a training plan and follows it faithfully. She looks for opportunities to swim against strong swimmers in order to prepare for swim meets. She does whatever it takes not to fail when the pressure is on.

We have to embrace the occasional adversity that comes with our own divine training plan. We have a divine Coach to guide us in the Holy Spirit, to put us through our paces, for one reason: we need to endure.

Surround Yourself with Champions

Hebrews 12:1 begins with the word *therefore,* which means it is building on what came just before it in Hebrews 11—the chapter that lists the great and faithful saints of the Old Testament. Hebrews 12:1 calls those saints "so great a cloud of witnesses." Their exploits for God are being spoken to us as we read them in the Bible. Their trials and victories in faith serve as markers on our own faith journey. Because they endured and were faithful, so we can be. Because they made it, we know we can make it, too.

We need champions of the faith to encourage us. The Old Testament saints are great people to begin with, but we need living, breathing champions around us today as well as others who have gone before us. I love to read the biographies and accounts of faithful men and women of God who endured to the very end. We can learn how they did it and imitate their faithfulness.

And just a word of balance: I cited an Olympic athlete as someone we can learn from without a word about her spiritual life. In other words, people don't have to be outspoken Christians in order for you to learn principles that you can apply to your own life when it comes to training and enduring. Sometimes we're afraid to admit that we're reading a non-Christian or non-biblical book. Don't be! There are plenty of opportunities to learn from people apart from their spiritual choices that may be different from your own.

Find Your Passion and Pursue It

When your passion in life is clearly defined, it makes endurance easier. When there is something you really desire to attain, you will fight harder for it. (Like the apostle Paul's single-minded focus on pursuing Christ in Philippians 3:7–15.)

I recently read the biography of Eliezer Ben Yehuda, a Jew who devoted his life to the restoration of the Hebrew language to modern generations of Jews returning to their homeland of Israel. For forty-one straight years he devoted his life to this purpose. He wanted Jews returning to Israel from all over the world to adopt their mother tongue of Hebrew, which many generations had forgotten living in foreign lands. Until the restoration and Ben Yehuda's work on his sixteen-volume dictionary of Hebrew, the language was only used in religious contexts. He wanted it to become the everyday language of the Jewish people. And he lived to see his dream fulfilled. If you go to Israel today and find his grave, this is what you'll see written on his tombstone:

Here lies Eliezer Ben Yehuda, Faithful Fanatic.[1]

When I finished reading the story of this man's endurance, I wanted nothing less than to be a faithful fanatic for Christ! The word *fanatic* doesn't often convey a positive image—but I'm using it positively in this setting. I want to be a man who will endure anything to accomplish God's will in my life, as did the apostle Paul. In 2 Corinthians 11:23–27 we read of what Paul went through as he endured tribulations for the sake of Christ. Paul endured and taught Timothy to endure (2 Timothy 2:3). If we are focused on our calling in Christ, we can endure also.

Get Rid of What's Holding You Back

Back to the message of the writer of Hebrews: "Let us lay aside every weight, and the sin which so easily ensnares us" (Hebrews 12:1). Speaking of the Olympics, have you ever seen athletes run or swim in an overcoat and boots? Of course not! They lay aside every encumbrance and wear only what will make them go faster and farther.

We know that unbelief—a loss of trust in God—erodes our confidence in God. And I believe that's what happened to the recipients of the Hebrews letter. They were suffering and were afraid to go forward with their faith. They had forgotten what God had done for them in the past. They likely began doing something we sometimes do: they started feeling sorry for themselves. They forgot the lesson that Peter gave his readers: don't be surprised when difficult things happen (1 Peter 4:12). Their doubt and discouragement were like weights around their necks. They couldn't stay focused on the finished line with such weights dragging them down.

Encumbrances can become sins if we don't lay them aside. As Paul reminds us, "Whatever is not from faith is sin" (Romans 14:23). We must identify those things in our life that either are or have the potential to become sinful encumbrances that will keep us from enduring and winning the race. Don't just lay them aside temporarily; lay them aside for good. Get them out of your life the moment they appear so you can endure without entanglements.

Don't Even Think About Quitting

Hebrews 12:1 continues: "Let us run with endurance the race that is set before us." That little phrase—"let us"—occurs thirteen times in the book of

Hebrews. Those are words of exhortation if I ever heard them. The writer wants his audience to keep on: You can do this! Keep up! Let's go! Like a coach speaking to an athlete, the writer wants his readers not to give up. Yes, we depend on the grace of God for strength. But putting one foot in front of the other is up to us. Let us run with endurance!

The book *Grit* is about what makes people succeed. The author, Angela Duckworth, presents two points of view. One says successful people are born with the right genes and benefit from the right advantages in life. The other says success is mainly about your passion and perseverance—what the author calls "grit." The author wanted to know which of these templates is more true to life. After her testing and research, the author concluded it was number two. Grit, more than genes and advantages, is the key to success: "To be gritty is to keep putting one foot in front of the other. To be gritty is to hold fast to an interesting and purposeful goal. To be gritty is to invest, day after week after year, in challenging practice. To be gritty is to fall down seven times and rise eight."[2]

I liked one of the examples of people with grit she described—the actor Will Smith. He says, "The only thing that I see that is distinctly different about me is: I'm not afraid to die on a treadmill. I will not be outworked, period. You might have more talent than me, you might be smarter than me. . . . You might be all of those things . . . you got it on me in nine categories. But if we get on the treadmill together, there's two things: you're getting off first, or I'm going to die. It's really that simple."[3]

Stay Focused on the Goal

Finally, the key to everything is keeping our eyes on the goal. The *New International Version* of Hebrews 12:2 says it just that way: "Fixing our eyes on Jesus." Why? Because "for the joy set before him he endured the cross, scorning its shame, and sat down at the right hand of the throne of God." Jesus *endured* the cross and the shame in order to reach His goal—sitting down at the right hand of God. In verse 3, the writer uses Jesus as the example of how we ourselves need to endure: "For consider [Jesus] . . . lest you become weary and discouraged in your souls."

Jesus endured to reach His goal, and if we keep our eyes on Him and His example, we can endure and reach our goal of finishing the race set before us. Again, it is God's power working within us that makes it possible. Yet we are exhorted to do the work ourselves: "strengthened with all might, according to His glorious power, for all patience and longsuffering with joy" (Colossians 1:11). We need God's power in us in order to endure.

In his book *Good to Great*, Jim Collins tells the story of a championship high school cross-country team that based their success on a simple idea: run the best at the end. Their runners didn't try to lead every race until the end, when they overtook their competitors and won. It's such a simple idea, but that idea was drilled into the thinking of all their coaches and runners: run your best at the end.[4]

I believe we are near the end of our time here on earth. I don't know when Christ is going to return, but I do know we get closer every day (Romans 13:11), and I do know that I want to run strong at the end. I hope you do as well. To do so, "You have need of endurance" (Hebrews 10:36).

APPLICATION

Personal Questions

1. When you are greeted by difficult times in your life, do you usually want to surrender or push forward in endurance?

   What hardships are you facing that may be causing you to want to give up the fight?

2. Often, God teaches us endurance through adversity. Read James 1:2–4 and Romans 5:3–4. How do these passages encourage you to persevere through adversity?

3. You can learn endurance by surrounding yourself with champions— people whose trials and victories in faith serve as markers on our own faith journey.

a. Read Hebrews 11. What types of trials did the people listed in this chapter endure? How were they able to overcome them?

b. Is there anyone in your life who inspires you with their refusal to give up? If not, can you be the person who inspires others with your determined endurance?

4. What's holding you back? Do some self-examination.

a. Is unbelief hindering you?

b. Is some habit stalling your spiritual momentum? Is some sin demoralizing you?

c. What change do you need to make if you're going to keep going in the strength of the Lord?

5. Read Hebrews 12:2.

a. According to this verse, what's the key to living a life of endurance?

b. How did Jesus model endurance?

c. Take a few minutes to "fix your eyes on Jesus" and His endurance. Ask God to make you a person of endurance. Commit yourself to never giving up when you are faced with the trials of life.

Group Questions

1. Do you find the smaller problems you confront every day more difficult to deal with than the major problems that appear every so often? Why or why not?

2. Hebrews 10:36 says we have need of endurance. Discuss some reasons why endurance is necessary for a godly life.

3. Read James 1:2–4 and talk about the following questions:

   a. Has God promised us a life of comfort?

   b. Rejoicing through tribulation is easier said than done. What steps can we take to see the positives to hardships? Why can we have joy in adversity?

   c. According to verse 4, what is one positive outcome to successfully enduring the trials of life?

4. One way we learn endurance is by "surrounding ourselves with champions."

   a. List some people, alive or deceased, who inspire you to continue running the race with endurance.

   b. Who are some people in the Bible who modeled endurance? Retell their stories to the group.

5. Read Hebrews 12:2.

   a. According to this verse, Jesus endured the cross by keeping His eyes on the goal. What was His goal?

b. Why do you think that focusing on a goal helps us endure difficult circumstances?

6. Spend a few minutes praying Colossians 1:11 over each member of the group. Ask God to strengthen each person "with all might, according to His glorious power, for all patience and longsuffering with joy."

DID YOU KNOW?

While there are numerous kinds of endurance races held all over the world, none is as mysterious as the Barkley Marathon held in Frozen Head State Park near Wartburg, Tennessee. While it is quirky, that doesn't mean it isn't hard. Out of the more than 800 times entrants have started the race, it has been completed in the allotted time only eighteen times by fifteen runners. The annual race is limited to forty runners who must cover five unmarked twenty-mile loops—a total of 100 miles in less than sixty hours. The race basically consists of running up and down rugged, wooded mountains—nearly 55,000 feet of vertical climbing. The race is not advertised, and there is no website. It is held in March or April, and the people who enter somehow find out when and where.

Notes
1. Robert St. John, *Tongue of the Prophets: The Life Story of Ben Eliezer Yehuda* (New York: Doubleday, 1952), 367.
2. Angela Duckworth, *Grit: The Power of Passion and Perseverance* (New York: Scribner, 2016), 275.
3. Ibid., 46.
4. Jim Collins, *Good to Great* (New York: HarperCollins, 2001), 206.

A Life of Compassion

LUKE 10:25-37

In this lesson we discover the true meaning of compassion.

It is not enough to recognize and bemoan the abundance of needs in the world. It is only enough when we see a need that God has shown us and act to help meet that need as best we can. Only then have we fulfilled the dual commands of Scripture to love God and our neighbor.

OUTLINE

   I. Compassion Is Not Academic

  II. Compassion Is Not Abstract

 III. Compassion Is Not Afraid

 IV. Compassion Is Not Analytical

  V. Compassion Is Action
     A. Compassion Is What We See
     B. Compassion Is What We Do
     C. Compassion Is How We Do It
     D. Compassion Is How Much It Costs Us

OVERVIEW

Compassion can be exercised in many venues and for many reasons. But the greatest revelation of the kind of person we are usually happens "in the moment." When life presents a moment to us, the fruit of the Holy Spirit is demonstrated spontaneously because we are submitted to the lordship of Christ in our life.

Compassion is certainly like that. We may round a corner in life and be suddenly confronted with a situation of great need. The need could be for money or food or clothing or encouragement or justice or something else. They are the kinds of situations Jesus encountered every day during His public ministry. Now, we are the hands and heart of Jesus on this earth. The fruit of the Spirit is given so we might respond as He would. Jesus wants to be compassionate through us.

A moment that brought forth compassion for a needy stranger is nowhere better illustrated than in the parable of the Good Samaritan (Luke 10:25–37). I believe this is the greatest story of compassion found in the Bible. This story gives us both sides of the compassion coin: how *not* to respond with compassion and how *to* respond with compassion. It is up to us to choose which example we will follow.

Compassion Is Not Academic

Compassion is not academic, but the reason Jesus told the story of the Good Samaritan arose out of an academic question asked by a lawyer—a question designed to test Jesus. The lawyer asked, "Teacher, what shall I do to inherit eternal life?" (verse 25) This lawyer was not like modern lawyers; he was a man who was an expert in the Mosaic Law. He was more like an ancient theologian than a modern lawyer; he was a professional student of the Old Testament.

Jesus answered with a question of His own: what does the Law say? And the lawyer answered correctly: love God and love your neighbor. And Jesus commended his answer. But then the lawyer asked the question that prompted Jesus to tell the story. The lawyer asked (still wanting to catch Jesus in a theological compromise), "And who is my neighbor?" (verse 29). This gave away his heart. He knew what the Law said, but he didn't live it out in his life. If he was used to loving his neighbor, he would know who his neighbor was. Jesus turned the tables on him by telling the story.

Jesus didn't allow the lawyer to turn "neighbor" into an academic definition about Jew versus Gentile or some other set of distinctions. That's because compassion isn't an academic debate. Compassion is an act of the heart. The definition of "neighbor" Jesus was about to unveil would be unlike anything this legal scholar and his friends had ever considered. As one of my seminary professors, Haddon Robinson, once put it, *My neighbor is a person with a need I can meet.*

Obviously, Jesus didn't say those words. Instead, He led the lawyer, and all those listening, down the path of self-discovery. He wanted *them* to define neighbor, not define it for them. And He wants us to make the same discovery. We all have a bit of the academic lawyer in us, by which we treat the Bible and theology as arms-length subjects instead of heartfelt convictions. When it comes to compassion, Jesus wants us to be the ones who demonstrate it in His name.

Compassion Is Not Abstract

Jesus began His story with a subject with whom it was easy to identify: a man traveling from Jerusalem to Jericho who was attacked by thieves who robbed him, wounded him, and left him for dead (verse 30). This was not an abstract image; it was commonplace. The road connecting Jerusalem and Jericho was a favorite haunt for thieves—seventeen miles of narrow, twisting road in the Judean wilderness. But Jerusalem and Jericho were both busy cities, so there was constant traffic on the road. Jesus' listeners knew the situation well; they might have wondered if Jesus' story was true, it was so realistic.

When the lawyer asked, "Who is my neighbor?" Jesus painted a picture of a beaten, wounded, robbed, innocent traveler. The question then became, "Is this man my neighbor or not?" Jesus was about to demonstrate why the lawyer might be inclined to answer "no"—and why he would be wrong.

Compassion Is Not Afraid

In Jesus' story, an innocent Jewish man is lying beaten and wounded by the side of the road. So Jesus had a priest come down the road—someone the lawyer could identify with as a member of the upper levels of Jewish society (verse 31). And the priest passed right by the man on the other side of the road. We don't know for sure, but it's possible this priest was heading from Jericho to Jerusalem to serve his allocated two weeks of service in the temple. In other words, he was going to perform religious duty and couldn't be distracted by a dying man.

The priest was likely afraid of what stopping might mean: delay, inconvenience, financial cost, and, most of all, ceremonial uncleanness if he touched a dead person. His uncleanness would have lasted seven days, and he would not have been able to serve in the temple. The cost was too great. He was afraid helping this wounded man would negate the one chance he had that year to serve in the temple in Jerusalem. Religion took precedence over a needy person.

Charles Swindoll tells a story of some seminary students who were studying this same passage from Luke in a Greek class. A few of the students decided to do a test. They dressed one of their group in torn, "bloody" clothing and had him lay outside one of the seminary buildings as if he'd been attacked. It was a test; they wanted to see if any of the other students would stop to help him. And none did. Students knew the Greek text of the Good Samaritan story but had no idea how to apply it. Religion took precedence over a "needy" person.[1]

First John 3:17–18 says that people who have the ability to help others but fail to do so lack the love of God.

Compassion Is Not Analytical

After the priest passed by, a Levite came down the road (verse 32). Levites were not descendants of Aaron and therefore not priests, but they were still part of the religious leadership of the nation of Israel. Like the priest, the Levite knew the Old Testament well and the command to love one's neighbor. But he didn't stop. Like the priest, he calculated what it would cost to stop and decided, for whatever reason, the price was too high.

Both men illustrate the principle that there is a difference between true religion (caring for the needy—James 1:27) and doing religious work. The priest and Levite were religious workers who weren't involved in true religion.

Compassion Is Action

Having said what compassion is not—academic, abstract, afraid, and analytical—it is time to say what compassion is: action.

The third man to come down the road in Jesus' story was a Samaritan who took action (verses 33–35). He cleaned the man's wounds with oil and wine and bandaged them; he put the injured man on his donkey and took him to an inn and stayed the night, looking after him; the next day when he left, he gave the innkeeper additional funds to care for the man and promised to pay, upon his return, whatever else the innkeeper had to spend to take care of the man. That is what compassion looks like in action.

Jesus' story illustrated that the only person involved in this story whose actions demonstrated a true knowledge of God and His Word was the Samaritan. The Samaritan was the true neighbor. This would have outraged the lawyer and the fictional priest and Levite who were all Jews, because Jews *hated* Samaritans. Jews viewed Samaritans as half-breeds, the offspring of Assyrians who had settled in the north of Israel and Jews left in the land after the Assyrian conquest in 722 BC. Jews wanted nothing to do with Samaritans—and here Jesus was praising the actions of a fictional Samaritan who defamed two high-ranking Jews in the story. Jesus made a Samaritan the hero of a Jewish story.

There are four lessons to be learned from Jesus' story.

Compassion Is What We See

The Samaritan "saw him, [and] he had compassion" (verse 33). The priest and Levite saw the needy man with their eyes but not with their heart. It's easy to do; all of us, at times, are guilty of looking but not really seeing. We can't have compassion if we don't see people's needs. "But when [Jesus] saw the multitudes, He was moved with compassion for them" (Matthew 9:36). The same thing happened when Jesus saw another crowd (Matthew 14:14) and another (Matthew 15:32). When Jesus saw broken and needy humanity, He was moved with compassion. And the same was true of the Good Samaritan.

Compassion begins with seeing; compassion is drawn out of us by being around people who have needs. If we isolate ourselves from a needy world, we will never exercise compassion because we will never see the need for it. Studies on philanthropy have revealed that the wealthiest people rarely give money to humanitarian causes. Instead, they give to schools, hospitals, scientific research institutes, and the like. Why? Because those are the people they're around. They're never around poor and needy people; they've never *seen* them.

Compassion Is What We Do

After our eyes have been opened, compassion is what we do. I've already described the things the Samaritan did for the needy man—tangible, concrete, quantifiable actions (verses 34–35). He didn't just wish him well; he took steps to put him on the road to wellness.

There was risk involved in compassion—there almost always is. In the Samaritan's case, what if the robbers who committed the original crime were hiding beside the road waiting for someone to stop and help the man? It would have been a valid assumption that anyone stopping to help probably had money (which the Samaritan did). So the Samaritan put himself in harm's way for the sake of a needy person.

Think of how that might play out today. People who see someone lying in the street and needing help might call out, "I'm calling 911, man—hang in there! I can't stop; I can't get involved. But help will be here soon." Instead of risking getting dirty, bloodied, and perhaps being attacked oneself, some people would move on instead of stopping to help. But dialing 911 isn't the kind of help the Samaritan demonstrated. We can do better than that. Compassion demands actions that meet immediate needs. Compassion is what we see and what we do.

Compassion Is How We Do It

At the end of the story, Jesus asked the lawyer who he thought was the neighbor in the story. And the lawyer answered correctly: "He who showed mercy on [the needy man]" (verse 37). The Samaritan was the only one of the three passersby who showed mercy toward the wounded man. And mercy is evidence of compassion; mercy is revealed by neighbors.

What is insightful from this story is the fact that the Samaritan used what he had to help the needy person. He had oil, wine, cloth for bandages, a donkey, and money. Oil and wine were used commonly for medicinal purposes back then. It would be the equivalent of us pulling a first aid kit out of the trunk of our car to help an accident victim; pulling off our belt to create a tourniquet; using our cell phone to call for an ambulance; doing what we could to make the person comfortable; keeping them talking and conscious until medics arrived; paying to have their car towed home; and on and on. In other words, we do what we can, where we can, how we can, to help a person in need. We may not be able to meet every need the person has. But we can trust that what God has given us is all He expects us to use. And so we should.

Compassion Is How Much It Costs Us

There is almost always a cost that accompanies compassion. In the story, the Samaritan gave the innkeeper a down payment on the traveler's stay at the inn and promised to pay any balance due when he returned (verse 35). Love is costly. You cannot love and have compassion on others without it costing something: time, money, goods, services, emotions. True love is sacrificial; there is always a cost.

This story served as a rebuke to the over-confident, self-satisfied lawyer, and it should serve as a warning for us. If we see someone with a need and have to stop and calculate the cost to see if we're willing to help, then we've missed the point. Compassion is always costly. Spouses learn that love is costly, as do parents, friends, and loved ones. Perhaps most costly is the compassion we choose to demonstrate toward a stranger because we don't know where the story will end. We don't know what God has in mind in this encounter. So compassion requires faith as well.

After the lawyer answered correctly—that the Samaritan was the true neighbor—Jesus' words to him are His words to us: "Go and do likewise" (verse 37).

APPLICATION

Personal Questions

1. Would you consider yourself to be a compassionate person? Why or why not?

a. Describe a time when you showed compassion or witnessed an act of compassion.

b. Explain why compassion is often something that happens "in the moment."

2. Read the parable of the Good Samaritan in Luke 10:25–37. What do you think is the main point of the story?

3. The parable of the Good Samaritan gives us both sides of the compassion coin: how not to respond with compassion and how to respond with compassion. List and describe the four things compassion is not.

   •

   •

   •

   •

4. What is compassion?

   a. The Good Samaritan took action. List all of the things he did for the wounded traveler.

   b. Jesus made a Samaritan the hero of His story. Why is this surprising?

5. In this lesson you learned that compassion is about seeing. What is the difference between *looking* and *seeing* (verse 33)?

Ask Jesus to help you see those around you with His eyes—eyes that *see* with compassion.

6. In your life, who are your neighbors? Be specific.

In what ways can you help them? How can you turn compassion into action for them?

Group Questions

1. Have someone in your group describe a time when he or she showed compassion or witnessed an act of compassion.

As a group, ask people to share their definitions of compassion.

2. Read the parable of the Good Samaritan in Luke 10:25–37. Discuss what you think is the main point of the story.

3. Compassion is not academic. The lawyer at the beginning of the story was the equivalent of a modern-day theologian, but he did not show compassion to the wounded man on the road to Jericho.

   a. What is the difference between *knowing* God's Word and *understanding* God's Word?

b. Why do you think those who know the most about the Bible can be in danger of failing to show compassion?

4. Discuss as a group: *What is compassion?*

   a. List all the ways the Good Samaritan showed compassion.

   b. Why is compassion always costly?

5. What's the difference between *looking* at your neighbors and *seeing* them with eyes of compassion?

   a. Who are your neighbors? What are their needs?

   b. Take a few minutes to pray for the needs of your neighbors. And ask God to give you the courage and strength to help them in practical ways.

DID YOU KNOW?

As mentioned, the Jerusalem-to-Jericho road was a favorite haunt for thieves and brigands in Jesus' day. It was referred to as the "Way of Blood" because of the frequent attacks. The Jewish historian Flavius Josephus provides a clue as to why there might have been such an abundance of thieves in that day. King Herod had released some 40,000 workers who had been laboring on the temple and other projects. Many of these unemployed workers turned to thievery simply to stay alive after being let go from their construction jobs. It's another example of the connection between the New Testament and the time-and-space historical realities of the day.

Note
1. Charles R. Swindoll, *The Tale of the Tardy Oxcart* (Nashville, TN: Thomas Nelson, Inc., 1998), 105.

A Life of Generosity

SELECTED SCRIPTURES

In this lesson we explore how generosity to others demonstrates the goodness of God toward us.

One of the greatest mistakes anyone can make is to think they own anything. God is the creator and owner of everything. What we have has been given to accomplish His purposes, not ours. We are to be good stewards of His possessions; we are to be channels of His goodness to others.

OUTLINE

I. The Picture of a Generous Life

II. The Potential of a Generous Life

III. The Path to a Generous Life
 A. Change the Way You Think About Money
 B. Expose Your Heart to the Brokenness of Humanity
 C. Before You Do the Big Things, Do the Little Things
 D. Start Giving More Than You Can Afford
 E. Don't Be Afraid of Spontaneity
 F. Pray About Becoming a Radical
 G. Make Sure You're Moving Toward Your Treasure

OVERVIEW

There are many examples of generosity in the world. Whether it is a billionaire who purposes to give away all his money by the time he dies, a wealthy person or couple who establishes a foundation to do good to others, or a person who subsists on a menial wage yet manages to save a huge sum to give to charity upon his death, stories of generosity are all around us.

Generosity takes many forms, and it doesn't always involve money. There are many ways to do good; many ways to be generous. Respect, courtesy, forbearance, patience—all of these are expressions of a generous spirit. Each day you're given opportunities to exercise generosity of spirit: to respond to impatience with patience, to reply to a hurried or thoughtless comment with an expression of understanding or empathy, to overlook what you don't like in someone so you can seek and find what you do like. Generosity has a broad application.

In this lesson, I'm using the word *generosity* as a practical synonym for *goodness*, the actual word mentioned in Galatians 5:22 as part of the fruit of the Spirit. Good people are generous people, and generosity is more action-oriented than the more abstract idea of goodness. But they almost completely overlap as interchangeable ideas. In either case, goodness and generosity are traits that should be cultivated.

God is generous; from Him comes "every good gift and every perfect gift" (James 1:17). We, created in His image (Genesis 1:26–27), can be generous because He is generous toward His creation. In this lesson, we will look at the picture, potential, and path to a generous life as inspired by God Himself.

The Picture of a Generous Life

As is often the case, Jesus provided a beautiful example with which to illustrate to His disciples, and to us, what generosity looks like. It's found in Mark 12:41–44, a story of a poor woman putting her small coins into the temple treasury while wealthy people put in money from their abundance.

From historical records of the time, we know the temple had thirteen receptacles around the temple courts where people would deposit their monetary taxes, tithes, and offerings. Sitting in the temple courts, you could watch people of all socio-economic levels deposit their monies into the receptacles—funnel-shaped devices that guided the coins into a box beneath. There are even instances recorded of wealthy people bringing their money and exchanging it for the maximum number of small coins they could to make a big show of depositing great sums of money into the treasury as a gift for God.

One day when Jesus was there with His disciples, a poor widow came to deposit her offering. Based on the word *poor* in the Greek text, this widow was destitute, a beggar or pauper, having nothing. But in spite of having next to nothing, she put in "two mites" (verse 42). The amount she put in was worth very little in real, monetary value. But there was something important happening that Jesus wanted the disciples to see.

Jesus said the poor widow "put in more than all those who have given to the treasury" (verse 43). Somehow, her two tiny coins were "more" than the amounts put in by everyone else. She obviously didn't put in more real money than the others, so what did Jesus mean? Jesus' point to His disciples was that generosity is not determined by the amount given but by the sacrifice made. So, a poor widow's two tiny coins represented greater generosity than the much larger gifts given by others out of their poverty (2 Corinthians 8:1–4).

The Potential of a Generous Life

In short, generosity is not about the contents of your wallet but the content of your heart. Regardless of how much money we do or don't have, all of us have the potential to be radically generous if we have a generous heart.

In the Roman world, generosity was a virtue and responsibility of only the wealthy. They were patrons for artists and craftsmen, but their support always came with a *quid pro quo* attached. They wanted something in return for their generosity, or investment. So, it is against that backdrop—and the Roman influence in first-century Palestine—that the poor widow's gift is so striking. Even though every Israelite was expected to tithe, it would not have been surprising to find a desperately poor person claiming he or she had nothing to give. So, when she gave out of her poverty, Jesus declared her gifts to be greater than all the rest.

America has the potential to be a generous nation, and we are nationally. The U.S. government gives a lot of money away to various causes each year. But individually, more than eighty-five percent of Americans give away less than two percent of their income each year.[1] So I don't know if we can say America is a generous nation or not.

What about Christians? In one study, it was estimated that only ten to twenty-five percent of people in American churches tithe. The same study suggested that if the rest of the Church began to tithe, a large number of problems—hunger, death from preventable diseases, water and sanitation issues—would be eradicated and overseas mission work would be fully funded, with more than 100 billion dollars left for other ministry work.[2] If those numbers are accurate, then clearly the Church is not living up to its potential in terms of generosity.

The Path to a Generous Life

As with all the other fruit of the Spirit, the question should be asked: How do we cultivate generosity? How should a follower of Christ turn this gift of the Holy Spirit into Christlikeness in our personal life?

Change the Way You Think About Money

First, we need to change our perspective on money. We think our money is ours to do with as we will. But nothing could be more wrong. As cited above, every good and perfect gift comes from God (James 1:17). As David prayed, everything we have, including money, comes from God (1 Chronicles 29:14). Even the money we give to God comes from Him. We are simply managers, or stewards, of what He has given us to use for Him to accomplish His purposes. And there is one primary requirement of a steward: faithfulness (1 Corinthians 4:2). That means we don't do anything with God's gifts to us that is not consistent with His desires.

Yes, there is pleasure and joy in the gifts He gives. But we must remember that we are not owners of anything. Everything we have belongs to Him—time, talent, and treasure. So, when we hesitate to give generously because we hate to lose what is ours, just remember: it is not ours. It all belongs to God.

Expose Your Heart to the Brokenness of Humanity

Another way to adjust our perspective on generosity is to expose ourselves to the brokenness of humanity. Because of our prosperity in America, it's easy to forget how many people there are who don't have much at all.

Bill Gates, for many years the richest man in the world, recounted the event that pushed him and his wife to begin giving large amounts of money. He had visited a hospital in Africa that treated tuberculosis patients, after which he called his wife back in America. Choking up on the phone, he told her the hospital was a death sentence. It changed the Gates' lives. They purposed to use their money not to change one hospital but to impact the lives of millions of people at a time, which they have done.[3]

We will never develop a generous heart until we experience a broken heart . . . until, in the words of World Vision founder Bob Pierce, our hearts break over the things that break the heart of God.

Before You Do the Big Things, Do the Little Things

It's normal to think big when we get a new perspective in life. But most people can't start their own charitable foundation right off the bat. But remember: generosity is not about the contents of your wallet but the content of your heart. Far better to begin small than not to begin at all because you can't begin big.

For instance, start increasing the size of the tip you leave for hard-working servers in restaurants. Start buying candy or wrapping paper from the kids in your neighborhood who are raising money for their school. Consider giving something to the next person you see asking for money on the street—and ask God to show you how to do it lovingly and compassionately. Be a friend or encourager to someone who needs it. These are small acts of generosity, but they have this benefit: they help us develop a mindset of opening our hands and our heart and being a generous person.

Start Giving More Than You Can Afford

This one may be more of a challenge for some people: give more than you can afford. Nobody can tell you how much to give, but consider these words of C. S. Lewis on giving:

> I do not believe one can settle how much we ought to give. I am afraid the only safe way is to give more than we can spare. In other words, if our expenditure on comforts, luxuries, amusements, etc., is up to the standard common among those with the same income as our own, we are probably giving away too little. If our charities do not at all pinch or hamper us, I should say they [our expenditures] are too small. There ought to be things we should like to do and cannot do because our charitable expenditure excludes them.[4]

Generosity is one of the best ways to learn to "walk by faith, not by sight" (2 Corinthians 5:7). When we give within our budget or from our excess, it is not the same as giving more than we had planned. When we give more than we can afford, it usually means we cut back in some other area of life. And then we trust God to give us patience to do without something or trust Him to provide above and beyond what we expect—which He certainly can do (Ephesians 3:20).

Don't Be Afraid of Spontaneity

We definitely should be good stewards of the money God gives us through planning, saving, budgeting, and self-control. But we also must leave room for the Spirit of God to lead us into a situation we hadn't foreseen and learn to trust His guidance. Has the Holy Spirit put someone's need in our path in order for us to be generous and meet that need?

Proverbs 16:9 says, "A man's heart plans his way, but the LORD directs his steps." So, if you plan your day, or your year, and have things all figured out, you have to remember: your plans and God's steps may not always be the same thing. Do you believe God is in charge of your steps when He puts you in the presence of a neighbor with a need you can meet? Be spontaneous; let the Lord change your path to meet the need of another person.

Pray About Becoming a Radical

R. G. LeTourneau was a radical giver. In the first half of the twentieth century, he founded successful companies, held over 300 patents, funded Le-Tourneau College in Texas, gave generously to missionary enterprises in Africa and South America—and lived on just ten percent of his income. That's right—he "reverse tithed." Instead of giving away ten percent of his income and living on ninety percent, he did the opposite.

Obviously, he was a wealthy man to be able to live on just ten percent of his income. And most of us could not afford to do that. But "radical generosity" has nothing to do with the amounts; it has to do with the heart. What could you and I do to move toward radical generosity in our own life? Ask God for ideas on how to move from reserved to radical generosity.

Make Sure You're Moving Toward Your Treasure

Only two things in life are eternal: the Word of God and the souls of human beings. Everything else will perish when this earth is renovated and God establishes a new heaven and new earth. We want to make sure our treasure is heavenly treasure, not worldly treasure. When we die, we want to make sure our treasure is ahead of us in heaven, not left behind us on earth. Jesus said as much in Matthew 6:19–21 and summarized it this way: "For where your treasure is, there your heart will be also."

Generosity started with God and is to continue with us. God gives generously to us so we can be channels of His love and blessings to others—especially others who do not know Him at all. Open your hands and heart to others, and God will fill them.

APPLICATION

Personal Questions

1. Would you consider yourself a generous person? Why or why not?

    a. What is your motivation when you give?

b. Do you find it easy to be generous? If not, what gets in the way between you and generosity?

2. Read Mark 12:41–44.

    a. What was the issue with the wealthy? What was the purpose behind their giving?

    b. Who was more generous—the wealthy individuals or the poor widow? Why?

    c. Jesus used this story to make what point to His disciples?

3. The path to generosity begins with how you think about money. Do you think of money as a gift from God that is to be used according to His purposes? Why or why not?

    a. According to 1 Corinthians 4:2, what is the primary requirement of a steward?

    b. What are some ways you think God would have you manage His money?

4. In the journey toward generosity, it's far better to begin small than not to begin at all because you can't begin big. List some specific examples of little ways in which you can be more generous with your blessings.

5. "Radical generosity" has nothing to do with the amounts; it has to do with the heart. Spend some time in prayer, asking God to give you a heart of radical generosity.

Group Questions

1. What are some characteristics of a generous person?

   a. Do you think people are naturally generous? Why or why not?

   b. What are some common barriers to a life of generosity?

2. Discuss some of the examples of generosity in action in the New Testament.

   a. Who was the ultimate example of generosity? (2 Corinthians 8:9)

   b. How should we apply the story in Mark 12:41–44 to our lives?

3. Do we ever feel our money is *ours*? What does James 1:17 say about this?

4. What should the answer be to "how much should I give?"

   Discuss some of the sacrifices you might have to make if you begin giving sacrificially.

5. Read Matthew 6:19–21.

   a. Where are we to invest our treasure?

   b. What happens to earthly treasure? What happens to heavenly treasure?

   c. List some ways you can "lay up treasures in heaven."

   d. Verse 21 says that our hearts follow our treasure. Discuss.

6. Generosity started with God and is to continue with us. God gives generously to us so we can be channels of His love and blessings to others. Discuss some ways you and your group can model generosity to those around you.

DID YOU KNOW?

The whole idea of generosity in English terms derives from the Latin word *generosus,* which originally meant "of noble birth." It was a class thing—in the word *generous* is the word *genus*, which means "birth, race, or stock." So, a generous person was originally a person who was above average in his class, standing, and birth. The idea of acting generously gradually evolved as fitting behavior for those of noble birth. You may not have been born into a noble earthly family, but you were born again into the family of the King of kings. It therefore behooves us to give according to our noble standing.

Notes
1. Christian Smith and Hilary Davidson, *The Paradox of Generosity* (Oxford, UK: Oxford University Press, 2014), 102.
2. Mike Holmes, "What Would Happen if the Church Tithed?" *Relevant*, March 8, 2016, http://archives.relevantmagazine.com/god/church/what-would-happen-if-church-tithed.
3. Julie Bort, "Bill Gates Talks About the Heartbreaking Moment that Turned Him to Philanthropy," *Business Insider*, January 21, 2015, http://www.businessinsider.com/why-bill-gates-became-a-philanthropist-2015-1.
4. C. S. Lewis, *Mere Christianity* (New York: HarperCollins, 1980), 144–145.

A Life of Integrity

SELECTED SCRIPTURES

*In this lesson we discover what integrity is and how to build
a life of faithfulness.*

The world is in desperate need of integrity, faithfulness, and loyalty. Those traits are so rare today that, when they are noticed, they stand out in the daily news cycle as being something surprising. In truth, integrity should be the norm that pervades and informs every area of our life.

OUTLINE

   I. The Rock of Integrity

  II. The Record of Integrity

III. The Road to Integrity
    A. Be Honest with Yourself
    B. Tell the Truth
    C. Keep Your Word
    D. Be Who You Are
    E. Avoid Bad Company
    F. Be Found Faithful
    G. Be Strong Under Fire
    H. Be Accountable to Someone

OVERVIEW

We don't have to look very hard to find dishonesty in the modern world. Unfortunately, we have to look hard to find examples of honesty, integrity, and faithfulness. Integrity is so rare that when it occurs it often makes the evening news or popular Internet news sites. Why is integrity news? Because we live in a world in which the end justifies the means. It's easy to convince ourselves that a dishonest word or action is okay because it may serve a greater good. We need more integrity in our world today, and Christians should lead that revival.

The *Oxford English Dictionary* defines *integrity* as "being honest and having strong moral principles." It offers a second definition: "the state of being whole and undivided," words that should call to mind several biblical principles (see Matthew 6:24).[1] "Undivided" suggests having all of one's life connected and integrated. We are not honest with one hand and dishonest with the other when it suits us. Integrity means we are consistent in our moral and spiritual approach to life.

In this lesson, we will look at the rock of integrity, the record of integrity, and the practical application—eight ways to travel the road to integrity.

The Rock of Integrity

Faithfulness is the biblical foundation for the modern idea of integrity, and it's the word Paul used when describing the fruit of the Spirit (Galatians 5:22).

Faithfulness is a manifestation of the Spirit because it is an attribute of God, who told Moses, "I AM WHO I AM" (Exodus 3:14). God is who He is; never changing, eternally the same. He has no past, present, or future. He lives in the eternal now and is always the same. The character of God is the rock of our faith: "He is the Rock, His work is perfect; for all His ways are justice, a God of truth and without injustice; righteous and upright is He" (Deuteronomy 32:4). Knowing God is to know the personification of integrity.

The Record of Integrity

In *The Seven Habits of Highly Effective People*, Stephen Covey says that integrity is "the value we place on ourselves." It is the ability to "subordinate your feelings, your impulses, [and] your moods to those values."[2]

Thirteen people in the Bible are specifically referred to as faithful people. And there are more obscure names than famous ones—which goes to show that God observes and notes faithfulness in everyone's life. As writer Rick Ezell says, "Integrity is not something we have, but something we are. It inevitably shows itself in what we do and say."[3]

Legendary investor Warren Buffett has said that when hiring people, you should look for three qualities: integrity, intelligence, and energy. Then he said, "If you don't have the first, the other two will kill you."[4] Integrity is the key to everything else; integrity makes all other traits worthy of honor.

The Road to Integrity

So, how do we develop integrity? There are eight on-ramps on the road to integrity.

Be Honest with Yourself

We have to be honest with ourselves before we can be honest with others. Integrity must start in our own heart before it can be extended to others. For example, Ted Williams, the great baseball player for the Boston Red Sox, once cut his own salary by twenty-five percent because he had been playing at what he considered to be a sub-par level. The team had always been generous and fair with him when it came to money, and he felt it was only right to do the same. So he docked his own pay![5]

As Christians, we have to tell ourselves the truth; we have to hold ourselves accountable; we have to be honest with ourselves. We forget that God sees all and knows all. He is as close as our breath and our thoughts. Do we really think we can be dishonest or lack integrity and God won't know about it? Psalm 139 is David's account of God's nearness to him and David's desire for God to search him and "see if there is any wicked way in [him]" (Psalm 139:24). David knew that God knew his heart; he wanted God to show him if there was any way he was not being honest about who he was.

Tell the Truth

I shouldn't even have to put such a basic exhortation in this lesson, but I do so because I know how strong the temptation can be *not* to speak the truth. It's this simple: God "cannot lie" (Titus 1:2), and therefore we should not lie. If we are created in His image and filled with His Spirit, then integrity in the form of truthfulness should be part of our life.

Someone has said that one of the benefits of telling the truth is that you don't have to remember what story you told to whom. That is, once stretching the truth starts, it leads to lie after lie after lie—and it gets very difficult to remember all those lies! Far better to simply speak the truth at all times and never worry about covering up what you've said. Your story is the same every time you tell it.

I'm not going to say that many Christians have a problem with outright lies. But many do have a problem with embellishing or exaggerating the truth. Even Christian leaders do when it comes to talking about the results of ministry efforts and things like church attendance. It's a dangerous game. God knows the truth—telling the truth is nothing more than saying what God would say.

Keep Your Word

Say what you'll do, then do what you say. That's an easy way to summarize what it means to keep your word. How many times do Christians say to others, "I'll be praying for you," versus the number of times they actually pray for that person? It's just a small example of how we give our word but may not always keep our word.

Again, God is our example. He is "the faithful God who keeps covenant [promises] and mercy for a thousand generations" (Deuteronomy 7:9). A thousand generations! Now that is keeping one's word. Even if circumstances change, God keeps His word to His people.

One of the American Vietnam POWs who was held for several years in the "Hanoi Hilton" prison defined integrity this way: "Integrity is keeping a commitment after the circumstances under which you made the commitment have changed." He had given his word to be loyal to America during peace time and was not about to change that commitment even in the midst of torture and suffering. Integrity means keeping your word forever.

Be Who You Are

A word often used in our cultural conversation is *poser*—someone who acts in an affected manner as a way of impressing others. Just as people pose for a portrait, a poser positions himself in such a way as to look attractive in spite of who he really is. We do not want to be posers; we want to be genuine, transparent people.

If we live a Spirit-filled life, manifesting the fruit of the Spirit, that will be an easy and welcoming way to live our lives. It's when we are not walking obediently with the Lord that we may try to give the impression that we are. The Bible has a word for that: *hypocrisy* (Romans 12:9). Philippians 1:10 says we should "be sincere and without offense"—be who we really are. *Sincere* comes from a Latin phrase in the Roman world, *sine cera*, or "without wax." It referred to vendors who sold ceramic or stone vessels or statues that had no cracks or blemishes covered over with wax. They were selling sincere goods—goods that were not hiding their true quality from the buyer.[6]

People of integrity are the real thing. They do not hide or cover up their faults. They don't try to give the impression they are something they are not.

Avoid Bad Company

First Corinthians 15:33 summarizes Proverbs 22:24–25 by saying, "Evil company corrupts good habits." Amy Rees Anderson summarizes the reasons for avoiding bad company:

> It is important to realize that others pay attention to those you have chosen to associate with, and they will inevitably judge your character by the character of your friends. Why is that? It is best explained by a quote my father often says when he is reminding me to be careful of the company I am keeping: "When you lie down with dogs you get fleas." Inevitably we become more and more like the people we surround ourselves with day to day. If we surround ourselves with people who are dishonest and willing to cut corners to get ahead, then we'll surely find ourselves following a pattern of first enduring their behavior, then accepting their behavior, and finally adopting their behavior. If you want to build a reputation as a person of integrity then surround yourself with people of integrity.[7]

Be Found Faithful

One of the clearest verses in Scripture about faithfulness is 1 Corinthians 4:2: "Moreover it is required in stewards that one be found faithful." The word *found* in this verse suggests a discovery made after careful observation. It suggests that God is looking at our lives, that He is looking for faithfulness—not just in finances, normally the subject of stewardship, but in every area of our life. It is wrong to think the biblical notion of stewardship applies only to money. Everything we have—not just our money—is a gift from God. We are to manage those gifts faithfully. As a property owner wants to see that his managers administer his property correctly, so God is looking for faithfulness in us, His stewards.

When my son worked as a scout for an NFL team, one of his jobs was to pick up players from the airport who were coming in to try out for the team. The coaches asked my son to make mental notes on the player's character as they drove from the airport to the stadium. What kind of person is he? What does he reveal about himself when he's "off the clock"? The coaches were looking for players with character—players who acted with integrity when the coaches weren't around. In the same way, God is looking to find us faithful *all the time*.

Be Strong Under Fire

Integrity—along with the rest of the fruit of the Spirit—is only proven when the temptation to do the opposite is present. So be assured: God will allow your integrity to be tested. Prepare now for those tests. Don't wait until the heat is on to decide whether you will be faithful or not, because the chances are good that you may not be. Settle this now in the quiet of the moment. Purpose to be a person of integrity no matter how hot the flames become.

Daniel and his three friends in Babylon proved their integrity. The story of Daniel's friends being threatened with being burned to death is a classic illustration (Daniel 3). They told the king that God was capable of delivering them, but even if He didn't they would not bow down and worship the king's idol. That was a decision they had made long before the moment arrived.

Joseph in Egypt is another example. He had been made the chief steward of a high official's household because of his integrity (Genesis 39). When the official's wife tried to seduce Joseph, he fled the scene, totally unwilling to compromise his integrity for the sake of a momentary pleasure. The wife accused him of attacking her, and he spent three years in prison.

That was the price he paid for his faithfulness. Decide today you will be faithful regardless of the cost.

Be Accountable to Someone

One of the best descriptions of accountability is in Hebrews 10:24–25, where we are exhorted to "stir up love and good works . . . exhorting one another." We need to be in relationships with faithful people, all of whom can hold each other accountable for integrity in words and deeds.

Megachurch pastor Bill Hybels tells a story of how he stopped by his church one evening for just a few minutes, parking in a "No Parking" zone. He thought it would be okay since he would only be there a few minutes. The next day, a member of the church's maintenance staff sent him a note saying others had seen his infraction and were not impressed. The staff member gently asked Pastor Hybels to set an example of parking in designated areas so as to encourage others to do so. And Pastor Hybels admitted the staff member was exactly on target. He had been wrong and was called to account. A small thing—but small choices of unfaithfulness can lead to larger ones. We need others to hold us accountable.[8]

The world and the Church need greater examples of integrity and faithfulness. That trend can begin with you as you travel the road to integrity.

APPLICATION

Personal Questions

1. Would you consider yourself to be a person of integrity? Why or why not?

   a. Either way, what are ways in which you can improve?

   b. Think of an example of genuine integrity that you have seen in your life—be it from a stranger or someone you know personally. What did that integrity look like?

2. Read Exodus 3:14 and Deuteronomy 32:4.

   a. How do these verses describe the faithfulness of God?

   b. How does God's faithfulness encourage you?

3. Reread the steps toward integrity described in the lesson. Which of the steps most challenges you? Why?

4. Think of some "under fire" moments in which your integrity might be tested. How can you react with integrity in such moments?

How can preparing for such moments help you not to compromise your integrity in moments of hardship?

5. Take a moment to be ruthlessly honest with yourself. What aspects of your life can you work on to become a person of integrity? Ask God to help you live a life of integrity.

Group Questions

1. Describe a time you were challenged to show integrity.

   a. Why is living a life of integrity so difficult? List three reasons.

-
-
-

b. In this lesson, what are some ways integrity is defined?

2. Read Exodus 3:14 and Deuteronomy 32:4. How do these verses describe the faithfulness of God?

   a. How does God's faithfulness encourage you?

   b. Ask people in your group to share specific ways they have experienced God's faithfulness.

3. List and discuss each step on the road to integrity. Talk about each step and what it fully entails.

   •

   •

   •

   •

   •

   •

   •

4. Warren Buffett once said, "In looking for people to hire, you look for three qualities: integrity, intelligence, and energy. And if you don't have the first, the other two will kill you." Discuss this quote. Why is integrity so important?

5. Read Hebrews 10:24–25.

   a. Have you found being accountable to others is helpful to your spiritual growth? Why or why not?

b. What are some blessings of accountability? What are some reasons we avoid it?

c. Discuss some ways you can "stir up love and good works"—and integrity—in each other's lives.

DID YOU KNOW?

John Wesley, the English evangelist and founder of Methodism, was once asked by a woman what he would do if he knew that at midnight the next night, he would die. Wesley thought about it for a minute and gave this surprising answer: "Why, just as I intend to spend it now. I should preach this night at Gloucester, and again at five tomorrow morning; after that I should ride to Tewkesbury, preach in the afternoon, and meet the societies in the evening. I should then repair to friend Martin's house, who expects to entertain me, converse and pray with the family as usual, retire to my room at ten o'clock, commend myself to my heavenly Father, lie down to rest, and wake up in glory."[9] In other words, John Wesley's life was lived on the cutting edge of integrity. That meant he had no great preparations to make in order to stand before God: no confessions, no repentance, no altering of his lifestyle. He lived a life that would commend him to God at any moment.

Notes
1. *Oxford Dictionary*, s.v. "integrity," accessed June 26, 2017, https://en.oxforddictionaries.com/definition/integrity.
2. Steven Covey, *The Seven Habits of Highly Effective People* (New York: Simon & Schuster, 2004), 157.
3. Rick Ezell, "Are You a Person of Integrity?" *Parenting Teens*, accessed June 22, 2017, http://www.lifeway.com/Article/Parenting-Teens-Are-You-a-Person-of-Integrity.
4. Warren Buffett, quoted in "Warren Buffett Looks for These 3 Traits in People When He Hires Them," *Business Insider*, January 4, 2017, http://markets.businessinsider.com/news/stocks/what-warren-buffett-looks-for-in-candidates-2017-1-1001644066.
5. Jerry White, *Honesty, Morality, and Conscience* (Colorado Springs, CO: NavPress, 1996), 18–19.
6. Ezell, "Are You a Person of Integrity?"
7. Amy Rees Anderson, "Success Will Come and Go, but Integrity Is Forever," *Forbes*, November 28, 2012, https://www.forbes.com/sites/amyanderson/2012/11/28/success-will-come-and-go-but-integrity-is-forever/#7eea725a470f.
8. Bill Hybels, "But I'm an Exception!" *CT Pastors*, Spring 1988, http://www.christianitytoday.com/pastors/1988/spring/88l2037.html.
9. John Wesley, quoted in J. B. Wakeley, *Anecdotes of the Wesleys: Illustrative of Their Character and Personal History* (New York: Carlton & Lanaham, 1870).

A Life of Humility

In this lesson we learn why pride is dangerous and humility is desirable.

Pride and humility (gentleness, meekness) are at opposite ends of the self-assessment scale. Pride is focused on self while humility is focused on God and others. Humility doesn't mean we should think less of ourselves. Rather, it means we should think of ourselves less.

OUTLINE

I. **Considering Humility**
   A. The Enemy of Humility
   B. The Example of Humility

II. **Cultivating Humility**
   A. Recognize Your Pride
   B. Start Serving
   C. Keep Listening and Learning
   D. Hang Out with Ordinary People
   E. Stop Taking Yourself So Seriously
   F. Spend Time with Children
   G. Don't Lose Perspective

OVERVIEW

Jim Collins is a former Stanford University professor and is now a management consultant and author. He conducted a five-year study to determine what moves companies from being "good" to "great" based on certain financial performance criteria. He found only eleven companies in the U.S. that met or surpassed certain performance goals. When he analyzed those eleven companies, he and his team discovered two traits common to all: steely determination and an attitude of humility. He wrote: "These leaders are a paradoxical blend of personal humility and professional will. They are more like Lincoln and Socrates than Patton or Caesar."[1]

Most people today equate meekness (humility) with weakness. But nothing could be more wrong. If the leaders of America's top companies display significant measures of humility, then humility can't equal weakness. Another misunderstanding is that humility equals self-deprecation—always trying to be humble and self-effacing instead of simply being genuinely humble. Sometimes self-deprecating (falsely humble) people put themselves down in front of others in the hopes of getting a compliment. It's a sad form of manipulation. We might all be guilty of that occasionally, but as a lifestyle it is not a sign of humility.

No one is born humble. That's why we are commanded to humble ourselves (James 4:10; 1 Peter 5:6–7). None of the nine traits of the fruit of the Spirit comes naturally to us. Anything the Spirit produces in us is not something we would do naturally—and that includes the fruit of gentleness, or humility. But, the positive side is that, if we are commanded to seek humility, it must be attainable.

As with other lessons in this series, we will first consider humility and then discover how to cultivate it.

Considering Humility

A definition of humility I really like is this: *Humility is the ability to use the power and resources I possess for the good of others.* Another well-known perspective is: *Humility is not thinking less of yourself; it is thinking of yourself less.* In short, humility is having a biblical understanding of ourselves.

The Enemy of Humility

The enemy of humility is pride: "Pride goes before destruction, and a haughty spirit before a fall" (Proverbs 16:18). We have all seen the truth of that statement in peoples' lives through the years; perhaps in our own life. One of my professors in seminary kept a record of seminary graduates who had either abandoned the faith or fallen into sin. He wondered if there was a common denominator that would link them together. He told me there was: all but one were men of pride or arrogance.

Is there something wrong with striving to be the best, with being recognized for our achievements? Not at all. But there is a thin line between wanting the best for God's glory versus our own glory. It all comes down to motivation. Why do we work hard and strive for excellence? Is it a matter of ego for us? Pride is a subtle enemy that can creep in at any time. If we grow to depend on the praise of other people, that means our happiness rests in others' hands. If we don't get praised we are deflated, humiliated, even angry. Our fallen human nature has to be propped up continually by all the wrong motivations.

As a pastor, I have occasionally gotten notes from people who were upset that I had not thanked them for some work or service or gift. While I always regret overlooking saying thanks when it is deserved, I'm sorry that people can find themselves upset when they're not thanked. That suggests their work or gift was not for the Lord but for themselves. Humility doesn't depend on recognition for happiness and contentment.

Pride has a ravenous appetite, needing constant feeding and affirmation. Humility, on the other hand, is self-sustained by the grace and blessing of God.

The Example of Humility

The greatest example of humility in human history is Jesus Christ. He left the glory of heaven to come to earth and assume the role of a servant to His own human subjects. It is no wonder that "He humbled Himself and became obedient to the point of death, even the death of the cross" (Philippians 2:8). Duane Elmer has captured Jesus' humility perfectly:

> The first earthly image we get of Jesus at the very beginning of
> his life is as a baby being born in a barn, surrounded by livestock.

The scene announces humility, lowliness, vulnerability, weakness, exposure. The last image we get of Jesus as he ends his earthly life is as a broken body hanging on a cross. The scene communicates humiliation, suffering, failure and, to many, defeat. Neither the opening nor the closing scenes of Jesus' life suggest anything but a life of humble service.[2]

Jesus certainly fulfilled the first definition of humility I cited in this lesson—using one's power and resources for the good of others. Jesus submitted His will to the will of His Father and exchanged His right to rule for the privilege of service.

Cultivating Humility

Paul wrote, "Let this mind [of humility] be in you which was also in Christ Jesus" (Philippians 2:5). How do we go about cultivating humility in our own life?

Recognize Your Pride

It takes humility to recognize our prideful tendencies; it's a lifelong quest, not a one-and-done experience. Every time we experience the grace that shows us a bit of pride in our life, we can know that we took another baby step toward humility (as long as we don't feel prideful about being wise enough to see our pride, and so on).

Like lots of addiction and dependency workshops, the first step is recognizing that we have a problem called pride. Paul warned the Christians in Rome "not to think of [themselves] more highly than [they] ought to think" (Romans 12:3). Paul then listed and discussed spiritual gifts in the Church, how all have their place and role. No gift is more or less important than another; no one should feel prideful over having what he considers a "better" gift than another.

One sure way to keep our pride in check is to have people around us who are willing to call us out when we are acting prideful or arrogant. The first thing in the list of seven abominations in God's sight is "a proud look" (Proverbs 6:16–17). We need people who will remind us of what pride looks like when we overlook it in our lives.

Start Serving

Paul gave one piece of evidence to illustrate the humility Christ displayed when He came to earth: He took "the form of a bondservant" (Philippians 2:7). There is a divine connection between humility and service. Jesus said of Himself that "the Son of Man did not come to be served, but to serve, and to give His life a ransom for many" (Mark 10:45). He also taught that greatness comes through service. In fact, there is a priority of promotion: servanthood before sainthood (Matthew 20:26–27; 23:11).

The world's idea of leadership is that leaders are at the top of the pyramid with all the servants below them. But in the kingdom of God, the pyramid is inverted; the leader is now at the bottom as the chief servant of everyone else. That's called servant leadership. Your eyes are taken off of you and put on those you are committed to serving.

Gaining a biblical perspective on our role in life will keep us humble. As Paul wrote leading up to his discussion of Christ and His humility, "In lowliness of mind let each esteem others better than himself. Let each of you look out not only for his own interests, but also for the interests of others" (Philippians 2:3–4).

Keep Listening and Learning

The overriding theme of the first ten chapters of Proverbs is the father instructing his son in the ways of wisdom. The father continually exhorts the son to hear, listen, and remember the words he is being given. In other words, prideful people are wise in their own eyes; they never feel they have anything to learn from God or others. How could anyone think they are too smart to learn from another person?

We should never get so old that we stop asking questions—and not just curiosity questions. We should remain willing to say, "I want to learn and acquire wisdom wherever I can." The best teachers are those who remain lifelong students. In fact, a sure sign of an educated person is one who increasingly realizes how much he or she doesn't know. In his book on humility, Pat Williams wrote:

> Humble leaders are always learning. They don't assume they have all the answers. They are humbly curious. They are always reading.

They listen to the ideas of people around them, including subordinates. They encourage fresh insights and suggestions from people at all levels, from board members to janitors.[3]

Hang Out with Ordinary People

Paul wrote this principle well in Romans 12:16: "Do not set your mind on high things, but associate with the humble. Do not be wise in your own opinion." The British pastor and commentator John Stott wrote, "Few kinds of pride are worse than snobbery. Snobs are obsessed with questions of status, with the stratification of society into 'upper' and 'lower' classes, or its division into distinctions of tribe and caste. . . . They forget that Jesus fraternized freely and naturally with social rejects, and calls his followers to do the same with equal freedom and naturalness."[4]

And speaking of John Stott—he was at a conference once where he was one of the main speakers. Before the conference started he struck up a conversation with a young pastor in attendance. They talked for quite some time before a friend of Stott's came by and greeted him by name. Only then did the young pastor realize he'd been speaking with the great John Stott as if he was just a regular person; Stott never implied, "I'm Dr. Stott—you should know who I am." That example of humility stayed with the young pastor from that point on.[5]

Stop Taking Yourself So Seriously

Can I tell you something I have learned? Nobody pays as much attention to us—whether our successes or our failures—as we think they do. We take ourselves far more seriously than anyone else does. And we shouldn't. We should develop the ability to laugh at ourselves.

When I visited a Christian bookstore once, the young female clerk at the counter was sort of watching me, I could tell. Shortly, she approached and said, "Are you who I think you are?" Before I could answer, she rushed to the back of the store and returned with another employee, carrying a stack of books. "Would you sign these books for us?" she asked, handing me six books by Josh McDowell! So I signed them all "Josh McDowell," happy to have made their day. I was honored to have been mistaken for someone like Josh McDowell. And it was a "humble pill" I gladly swallowed! Laughing at oneself is good medicine for the humble soul.

Spend Time with Children

We've all heard it: "Out of the mouths of babes!" This phrase originated in Psalm 8:2 and was repeated in the New Testament (Matthew 21:16). It is consistent with the idea we should become more like children if we want to enter the kingdom of God (Matthew 19:14; Luke 18:16). Not that children are sinless, perfect, or naturally humble—they aren't. But they have not been infected with the pride and arrogance that comes with competition, striving, and ambition in the world of adults. Children are relaxed and less self-conscious. If they fail or fall, they are not crushed with shame; their ego is not shattered. They are willing to pick themselves up and try again.

And sometimes children tell us exactly what we need to hear without thinking twice: "Daddy, you have a big stomach! Mom, you look tired!" Children can teach us about humility and keep us humble at the same time. The more time we spend with them, the better off we will be.

Don't Lose Perspective

Theodore Roosevelt, our twenty-sixth president, was a larger-than-life man. He loved the great outdoors, creating many national parks and monuments between 1901 and 1909. He went on safaris in Africa and helped open up that continent to the West. His biographers tell that one of Roosevelt's habits was to take White House guests outdoors late at night before retiring and have them stare up into the blackness of heaven, punctuated by stars. (This was before light pollution in big cities made it impossible to see the stars.) After he and his guests had contemplated the vastness of space for a couple minutes, he would say, "Gentlemen, I believe we are small enough now. Let's go to bed."

When the man who sits at the most powerful desk in the world is willing to contemplate his own smallness in light of God's vast universe, there is something of humility at work. Perhaps Roosevelt learned that lesson from King David of Israel, who expressed the same perspective in Psalm 8:3–5. And we would be well served to learn from them both.

May we experience the promise of James 4:10: "Humble yourselves in the sight of the Lord, and He will lift you up."

APPLICATION

Personal Questions

1. Would you consider yourself a humble person? Why or why not?

   a. Why do you think many people equate humility with weakness?

   b. Describe two misunderstandings of humility.

2. What is humility? List the two definitions of humility found in this lesson.

3. The enemy of humility is pride. Read Proverbs 16:18.

   a. According to this verse, where will pride lead you?

   b. List two other dangers of pride that are discussed in this lesson.

4. The greatest example of humility in human history is Jesus Christ. Describe Jesus' life of humility.

5. Write down seven ways you can cultivate humility in your life.

   -
   -
   -
   -
   -
   -
   -

a. Which of the seven most resonated with you? Why?

b. List two ways you can practice humility this week with those in your life—your family, your friends, and your acquaintances.

6. Read James 4:10.

a. When you humble yourself, what does the Lord promise to do?

b. Take a few minutes to prayerfully humble yourself before the Lord.

Group Questions

1. Discuss why humility is so difficult to cultivate in our day and age.

a. Describe the two counterfeits to true humility.

b. Discuss how Jesus was the greatest example of humility in human history.

2. What are the two definitions of humility described in this chapter?

Ask the people in your group which of the definitions they like best. Why?

3. Assign one of the seven strategies for cultivating humility to each person in the group. Give them a few minutes to review the strategy and then have them teach it to the group.

4. One sure way to keep our pride in check is to have people around us who are willing to call us out when we are acting prideful or arrogant. Discuss ways to do this in a respectful and loving way in your group.

5. Serving others is a powerful way to grow in humility. Read Philippians 2:3–4.

   a. How are we to think about other people?

   b. Brainstorm some ways you can look out for the interests of the other people in your group.

6. Read Psalm 8:3–5.

   a. How does the psalmist describe humility in these verses?

   b. Take a minute to contemplate both your smallness and your glory before God. How does this encourage you to pursue a life of humility?

DID YOU KNOW?

When someone says, "He made me feel like dirt" after a humbling experience, he is more right than he knows. The word *humility* comes from the Latin word *humus*, meaning soil or ground. The Latin adjective *humilis* then became "low" or "lowly"—a connection to the ground. Obviously, God doesn't want us to feel like dirt as the equivalent of humility. But it is ironic that "for dust [we] are, and to dust [we] shall return" (Genesis 3:19)—a good reminder that both our beginning and ending have their roots in the ground of lowly humility. Until, that is, God gives us a cloak of glory as our eternal inheritance (Romans 8:18).

Notes
1. Jim Collins, *Good to Great: Why Some Companies Make the Leap . . . and Others Don't* (New York: HarperCollins, 2001), 12–13.
2. Duane Elmer, *Cross-Cultural Servanthood* (Downers Grove, IL: InterVarsity Press, 2006), 22.
3. Pat Williams, *Humility* (Uhrichsville, OH: Shiloh Run Press, 2016), 93.
4. John Stott, *The Message of Romans* (Downers Grove: InterVarsity Press, 1994), 330.
5. Tim Chester, "The First Time I Met John Stott," July 28, 2011, https://timchester.wordpress.com/?s=stott&submit=Search.

A Life of Self-Discipline

*In this lesson we discover how and why we should win
the battle for a disciplined life.*

Self-control, or self-discipline, is the last fruit of the Spirit Paul mentions in Galatians 5. But, in a sense, it is the key to all the others. Self-discipline is that strength that allows us to do what we know should be done—like cultivate all the fruit of the Spirit. This trait is likewise a gift to be cultivated.

OUTLINE

I. The Battle for a Disciplined Life

II. The Blessings of a Disciplined Life

III. The Building Blocks to a Disciplined Life
 A. Embrace Your Dissatisfactions
 B. Beware of Good Intentions
 C. Start Working Out
 D. Talk Back to Your Body
 E. Fast Forward Your Life

OVERVIEW

Bestselling author Malcolm Gladwell chose the term "outliers" to describe some successful people and the reasons for their success. As Gladwell explains the apparent success of some and the apparent failure of others, he arrives at a very key conclusion. Whether it was hockey, music, computer skill, or the ability to make money, there is one thing all of the successful people had in common: they had all invested more than 10,000 hours of their life in learning to become what they were.[1] They were the products of self-discipline.

I believe self-discipline is the "outlier" that explains why some Christians seem to soar and others barely get off the ground. In Paul's description of the life beyond amazing (Galatians 5:22–23), the last character trait he lists is self-control. Its placement at the end of the list doesn't mean it's the least important. In fact, we might view it as the key to the previous eight traits Paul lists. Jesus indicated that self-control (denying yourself) was the first step in becoming His disciple (Mark 8:34–35). From beginning to end, the Christian life is about choosing Christ over the world—a choice that requires discipline.

The famous NCAA basketball coach Bobby Knight was controversial—but successful. He had a definition for self-discipline I have always liked: "Doing what you have to do, and doing it as well as you possibly can, and doing it that way all the time."[2]

Another author describes it this way: "The self-controlled person maintains progress toward a goal even when he is not in the mood, doesn't feel like making the effort, would momentarily enjoy something else or finds working toward his goal downright unpleasant."[3]

The New Testament word for self-control is a word used for "governing." Humanly speaking, self-control is about governing our desires and impulses, about governing ourselves—thoughts, emotions, actions—in a godly manner. The Bible suggests self-control touches our moods (Proverbs 25:28), our speech (Proverbs 13:3), our reactions (Proverbs 19:11), our time (Ephesians 5:15–16), our money (Proverbs 21:20), and our body (1 Thessalonians 4:4).[4]

But self-control is not something we do in our own strength; it is a gift from God, mediated by the Holy Spirit. Like all the other dimensions of the fruit of the Spirit, self-control is a gift that we must cultivate and actively pursue. We receive the gift and put it to use.

In this lesson we will look at the battle, the blessings, and the building blocks for a disciplined life.

The Battle for a Disciplined Life

At the heart of the battle for self-discipline is the internal war between the flesh and the Spirit of God (Galatians 5:17). That's for Christians, of course, but even non-Christians battle what they know to be right in their conscience and what they might otherwise want to do. It's a never-ending battle, often portrayed in cartoons as an angel perched on one of our shoulders and the devil on the other, both whispering in our ears at the same time.

The battle for a disciplined life goes all the way back to Eden, when Eve chose to disobey God's command not to eat the fruit of a certain tree. She was tempted by the serpent and was not able to control her desires—and we all know the result. Even the apostle Paul confessed to this battle raging in his own heart: "I don't really understand myself, for I want to do what is right, but I don't do it. Instead, I do what I hate. . . . I want to do what is good, but I don't. I don't want to do what is wrong, but I do it anyway" (Romans 7:15, 19, NLT).

The Bible is relevant for every age, but its description of the battle for a disciplined life is especially significant for ours. Daniel Akst, author of the book *Temptation: Finding Self-Control in an Age of Excess,* describes life in our modern Western culture as "a giant all-you-can-eat buffet, one that offers more calories, credit, sex, intoxicants, and just about anything else we can take to excess than at any time in history."[5]

The Blessings of a Disciplined Life

Self-control is rarely fun in the moment, but the results are always worthwhile. Think of people who train for a sport, save money for a car or house, or control their diet to reach a weight goal. Yes, the choices are hard, but the payoff is huge! Conversely, when we fail to make the choices we know we should, we suffer discouragement, even anger, which can lead to further lack of self-control. We say to ourselves, "Why bother?" With maturity should come increasing success in maintaining self-control.

In an April 2017 *Christianity Today* article titled "The Science of Sinning Less," sociologist Bradley Wright and psychiatrist David Carreon explained that research shows people with more self-control "live longer, are happier, get better grades, are less depressed, are more physically active, have lower resting heart rates, have less alcohol abuse, have more stable emotions, are more helpful to others, get better jobs, earn more money, have better marriages, are more faithful in marriage, and sleep better at night."[6]

The Building Blocks to a Disciplined Life

Let's look at five building blocks that can help us put together a disciplined life.

Embrace Your Dissatisfactions

Even the apostle Paul recognized that he had not accomplished his goal of following Christ as completely as he wanted (Philippians 3:12–13). He had been faithful; he had accomplished much for the Lord. But he was dissatisfied in a sanctified sense. The more he accomplished for Christ, the more he wanted to do. He used his dissatisfactions to spur him on to greater commitment and self-discipline.

How could one of the most important people in Christian history, apart from Christ Himself, have considered his commitment and pursuit of Christ to be lacking? It was simply because he had the hunger and thirst for righteousness Jesus described in the Beatitudes: "Blessed are those who hunger and thirst for righteousness, for they shall be filled" (Matthew 5:6). The blessing is not for the righteous; it is for those who hunger and thirst for righteousness.

I remember when I realized that being dissatisfied with my spiritual progress was not a bad thing. Instead, it was a good thing! Hunger and thirst makes us pursue that with which we can be filled. We should enlist our dissatisfactions to drive us toward great self-control for Christ and His kingdom. We will never see the need for the rigors of self-discipline if we think we have arrived, regardless of the area of life we are talking about. Only those who want more will subject themselves to the demands of self-control.

More than one motivational speaker that I have listened to over the years has expressed this maxim: "Change happens when the pain of staying the same is greater than the pain of change."

Beware of Good Intentions

It's easy to think that wanting to do better is the same as doing better. When I was younger, I was enthralled with the exploits of many spiritual leaders and missionaries. Only later did I realize I couldn't be like them simply by reading about them. Proverbs 12:11 and 28:19 warn against living in a fantasy world. Such a person "is devoid of understanding" and "will have poverty enough!"

The British commentator William Barclay, in his commentary on the Gospel of Matthew, tells of a person who never translated desires into accomplishment by exercising self-control:

The poet Samuel Taylor Coleridge is the supreme tragedy of indiscipline. Never did so great a mind produce so little. He left Cambridge University to join the army; he left the army because, in spite of all his erudition, he could not rub down a horse; he returned to Oxford and left without a degree. He began a paper called *The Watchman* which lived for ten issues and then died. It has been said of him: "He lost himself in visions of work to be done, that always remained to be done. Coleridge had every poetic gift but one—the gift of sustained and concentrated effort." In his head and in his mind he had all kinds of books, as he said himself, "Completed save for transcription. I am on the eve of sending to the press two octavo [the book form] volumes." But the books were never composed outside Coleridge's mind, because he would not face the discipline of sitting down to write them out. No one ever reached any eminence, and no one having reached it ever maintained it, without discipline.[7]

Start Working Out

Paul gave young Timothy, his pastoral protégé, some wise counsel concerning spiritual growth: Reject worldly distractions and "exercise yourself toward godliness" (1 Timothy 4:7). "Exercise yourself" sounds like the kind of self-control athletes and musicians use to reach their goal: practice, improve; practice, improve; practice, improve!

Paul wanted Timothy to train himself to be godly. We've seen the word *exercise* or *train* before in this series; it comes from the Greek word from which we get *gymnasium*. In other words, spiritual growth and godliness is no easier than becoming an athlete. It takes training and exercise daily. Paul wrote something similar to the Philippians: "Work out your own salvation with fear and trembling" (Philippians 2:12). "Work out" here does not mean exercise, but it is just as relevant. It refers to producing results, completing a task, doing what is needed—all of which requires self-control.

Peter reminded his readers that they had been given "all things that pertain to life and godliness" including "great and precious promises" (2 Peter 1:3-4). But Peter did not allow them to rest on their spiritual inheritance. Quite the contrary. In the next three verses, he tells them to be diligent to acquire faith, virtue, knowledge, self-control, perseverance, godliness, brotherly kindness, and love (verses 5–7). The word "diligent" could be translated as "make every effort." He wanted to make sure they understood the challenge of following Christ. Godliness does not happen easily, automatically, or overnight.

Tom Landry, longtime coach of the NFL Dallas Cowboys, said, "The job of a football coach is to make men do what they don't want to do in order to achieve what they've always wanted to be." That's a fair description of the Christian life. We want to be like Christ, but it takes self-discipline to get there.

Talk Back to Your Body

In one of his most illustrative passages about the spiritual life, Paul likens it to an athletic event. In a big contest, he writes, all run the race but only one wins the prize. Greek and Roman athletes competed for perishable prizes, but "we for an imperishable crown." Therefore, Paul says, "I discipline my body and bring *it* into subjection, lest, when I have preached to others, I myself should become disqualified" (1 Corinthians 9:25, 27). Paul was unwilling to avoid the hard work he exhorted others to undertake and endure. He wanted to cross the finish line as a faithful steward of the grace of God in his life; nothing else was acceptable. He wanted the imperishable crown being held in reserve for all who are faithful in Christ.

The older I get, the more this passage resonates with me. There are just some days when my body is telling me that it doesn't want to obey me anymore. I actually have arguments with my body. I talk back to it! My body wants to sleep; I need to get up! My body wants to eat; I have already eaten enough! My body wants to stop exercising; if I stop I might not ever start again. My body resists the effort necessary to pray and read the Bible; I cannot let my body win this battle. My body wants to give up when the going gets tough; but I know I must go on.

Sometimes life is like riding a bicycle into a gale-force wind. Every pedal stroke requires monumental effort. We know if we don't continue, one stroke at a time, we will not finish. And so we continue on—the idea of not crossing the finish line, of losing our reward, keeps us going.

Fast Forward Your Life

Goals are powerful; they pull us out of the present and propel us into the future. The writer to the Hebrews transitioned from the present to the future in Hebrews 12:1–2: "Let us lay aside every weight . . . and let us run with endurance the race . . . looking unto Jesus, the author and finisher of our faith."

Jesus is our goal; Jesus is our future. In the present, we lay aside sin and its entanglements so we can keep pressing forward into the future to be conformed to the image of Christ (Romans 8:29). Such complete conformity will not happen in this life, but we get closer each day that we pursue it. Like Paul, we do not want to fail to cross the finish line faithfully. And it is the knowledge that we will "see Him as He is" (1 John 3:2) that pulls us forward into the future. Man cannot survive without a goal and the hope of reaching it. Such attainment gives us every good reason to live a disciplined life.

You know you are in the battle. Consider the blessings and use the building blocks to build the godly life you desire through the gift of self-discipline.

APPLICATION

Personal Questions

1. After studying this lesson, do you feel you are a disciplined person?

   a. Are you able to govern yourself? Explain.

   b. Do you make decisions based on what you know is right or how you feel at the time?

   c. What temptations do you struggle with most?

2. What was your favorite definition of self-discipline in this lesson? Consider writing it on an index card and reviewing it every day this week.

3. Look up the following verses and describe the areas of your life that should be under control.

   Proverbs 13:3

   Proverbs 19:11

   Proverbs 21:20

   Proverbs 25:28

   Ephesians 5:15–16

   1 Thessalonians 4:4

4. Self-discipline is rarely fun in the moment, but the results are always worthwhile. List some of the blessings of a self-disciplined life.

5. Below are the five building blocks to self-discipline. For each building block, list the key verse and write out a one-sentence summary:

  a. Enlist your dissatisfactions.

  b. Beware of good intentions.

  c. Start working out.

  d. Talk back to your body.

  e. Fast forward your life.

Group Questions

1. Discuss why self-discipline is so difficult.

  a. Why is it so important?

  b. What are some results of an *undisciplined* life?

2. Ask three people to share their favorite definition of self-discipline from the lesson. Have them explain why it was so significant to them.

3. When you think of self-discipline, do you think of the pain involved in it or the blessing that results from it? Discuss.

  a. What are some of the blessings of a disciplined life?

  b. Ask someone to share a time when self-discipline brought them a blessing.

4. Discuss each of the five building blocks to a life of self-discipline. Look up the key verses for each one.

5. Self-discipline is a battle that is best pursued with the help of others. Spend some time praying for one another, asking the Holy Spirit to give you the strength to live a disciplined life.

DID YOU KNOW?

The word Paul uses for *discipline* in 1 Corinthians 9:27 ("discipline my body") is a rare word—and a graphic one (occurring elsewhere only in Luke 18:5). It is based on a Greek word that referred to the part of the face just beneath the eyes—the area of the cheekbones. And it meant to strike a person in the face until they were brought into submission. In verse 26, he even refers to the image of men boxing one another, saying he was going to strike for effect! So, Paul was being graphic and serious about his need (and our need) to discipline himself so as to win the race set before him.

Notes
1. Malcolm Gladwell, *Outliers* (New York: Hachette Book Group, 2008), 38–39, 143–144.
2. Bobby Knight, quoted in Frank Deford, "The Rabbit Hunter," *Sports Illustrated,* January 26, 1981, https://www.si.com/vault/1981/01/26/825311/the-rabbit-hunter-bobby-knight-may-be-tremendously-successful-on-the-court-but-off-it-indianas-controversial-basketball-coach-often-stalks-the-insignificant.
3. William Backus, *Finding the Freedom of Self-Control* (Bloomington, MN: Bethany House Publishers, 1987), 36.
4. Adapted from Rick Warren, "Developing Biblical Self-Control," *Pastor Rick's Daily Hope,* May 21, 2014, http://pastorrick.com/devotional/english/developing-biblical-self-control.
5. Daniel Akst, "We Have Met the Enemy," *The New York Times,* December 30, 2010, http://www.nytimes.com/2010/12/31/books/excerpt-we-have-me-the-enemy.html.
6. Bradley Wright with David Carreon, "The Science of Sinning Less," *Christianity Today,* April 21, 2017, http://www.christianitytoday.com/ct/2017/may/science-of-sinning-less.html.
7. William Barclay, *The Gospel of Matthew, Volume 1* (Louisville, KY: Westminster, 1958), 284.

A God-Inspired Life

In this lesson we discover how dependence on the Holy Spirit is the only way to manifest the fruit of the Spirit.

Everything depends on power—homes, cities, transportation, even our human body. But we have a need for spiritual power as well. We have been given the gift of an amazing life to live, but how will it be powered? By the indwelling Holy Spirit—the source of all spiritual fruit and gifts.

OUTLINE

I. Living a Life Empowered by the Holy Spirit

II. Living a Life Engaged with the Holy Spirit
   A. Desire the Spirit
   B. Denounce Your Sin
   C. Devote Yourself to God's Word
   D. Die to Your Own Ambition
   E. Determine to Commit to the Spirit's Direction
   F. Don't Quit, Keep Playing

OVERVIEW

It was 1979, and Donna and I were happily leading the Blackhawk Baptist Church in Fort Wayne, Indiana. The church was growing and expanding its ministries, and we had no reason to think about leaving. Then a man named Tim LaHaye told me I was going to be the next pastor of the Southern California church he had led for twenty-five years.

I resisted the idea of leaving Indiana for two years while Donna and I talked and prayed about the opportunity. Long story short, we decided to yield to what appeared to be God's clear leading. And that decision to submit to the Holy Spirit changed everything in amazing ways we couldn't have imagined.

In this series of lessons, I have encouraged you to make nine decisions that will transform your life. But behind each of these decisions is one that impacts all of the others: what will you decide to do with the Lord Jesus Christ? He came into this world to give us the most abundant life possible (John 10:10)—a life beyond amazing. But we must give Him our life in order to experience the life He has for us.

In his letter to the Galatian believers, Paul describes this life as a fruitful life (Galatians 5:22–23). In lessons two through ten in this series, we have examined nine traits of a fruitful life—a life empowered and produced by the Holy Spirit. In this lesson, I want to focus on the Holy Spirit Himself and how He produces this life beyond amazing.

Living a Life Empowered by the Holy Spirit

On February 10, 2013, a fire broke out in an engine room of the Carnival cruise ship *Triumph,* which knocked out the ship's power. The power outage shut down all services on the ship; it drifted for four days before being towed into port at Mobile, Alabama. The 4,200 passengers and crew debarked hungry, smelly, exhausted, and newly impressed with the results of a power outage on modern life.

The Holy Spirit is the Christian's spiritual power source; it is why Paul commands us to be "filled with the Spirit" (Ephesians 5:18). We cannot manifest or enjoy the fruit of the Spirit if the Spirit does not have control of our life.

Jesus is the only person who has manifested the fruit of the Spirit perfectly. To do so in His humanity, He had to depend on the Spirit just as we do. As He told His disciples, "The words that I speak to you I do not speak on My own authority; but the Father who dwells in Me does the works" (John 14:10). Jesus was full of the Spirit (John 3:34). Following His lead is the only way to live a life beyond amazing.

Living a Life Engaged with the Holy Spirit

It is true that the Holy Spirit indwells every believer when he or she is saved (Acts 2:38; 1 Corinthians 10:12–13). But that doesn't mean we are to be passive in that relationship. As you have read in these lessons, we must cultivate the fruit of the Spirit as our relationship with Him matures. Here are six ways to live a life engaged with the Holy Spirit.

Desire the Spirit

At the climax of one of Israel's festivals, Jesus stood up in the temple and said, "If anyone thirsts, let him come to Me and drink" (John 7:37). The next verse tells us that He was speaking of thirsting for the Holy Spirit. Although the Holy Spirit wants to direct our lives, He doesn't override our free will or seize control of our minds. Rather, He sets the direction and gives us power and wisdom, but it is up to us to desire His guidance, gifts, and fruit.

John Stott had the practice to begin each morning with this prayer, a confession of his desire for the Holy Spirit's help in his life: "Heavenly Father, I pray that this day I may live in your presence and please you more and more. Lord Jesus, I pray that this day I may take up my cross and follow you. Holy Spirit, I pray that this day you will fill me with yourself and cause your fruit to ripen in my life: love, joy, peace, patience, kindness, goodness, faithfulness, gentleness and self-control."[1]

Denounce Your Sin

Because the Holy Spirit is holy, He cannot thrive in a sinful environment. But when we repent of our sins—confess and turn away—we are forgiven and cleansed (1 John 1:9). As cleansed vessels, the Holy Spirit can fill us and guide us into God's will for our life. When we are forgiven, we are cleansed of the offensive presence of sin.

Devote Yourself to God's Word

Salvation is not an end but a beginning. It's the starting line of a lifelong process called sanctification—the conformation of our image into the image of Christ (Romans 8:29). We study the Word of God to discover His general will and for the Spirit to quicken to us individual points of guidance. If we are to "be ready for every good work" (Titus 3:1), we must have stored up the truth of God that the Spirit can call to mind when needed.

It's like using our computer: data is stored on the hard drive, available for the operating system to use. When we fill our mind—our hard drive—with the data of God's Word, the Spirit can put it to use in our life. We must continually be taking in the truths of God's Word in order to be conformed to Christ by the Spirit's power.

Die to Your Own Ambition

In the verses that immediately follow the listing of the fruit of the Spirit, Paul says, "And those who are Christ's have crucified the flesh with its passions and desires. If we live in the Spirit, let us also walk in the Spirit" (Galatians 5:24–25). Crucifying the flesh is a daily challenge—choices and decisions to submit to God's righteousness instead of our unrighteousness. Yielding to the Spirit instead of going our own way. We have to crucify our will in order to follow Christ (Matthew 16:24–25). "No servant can serve two masters" (Luke 16:13). Your life has no room for two CEOs. Either you will be in charge or you can place the Holy Spirit in charge. The Holy Spirit is the only one who can lead you into a life filled with the nine attributes we've been examining in this series.

There is a story about a bird flying along the coast of Norway when a powerful storm suddenly arose and blew her out over the North Sea. The bird fought hard against the storm, trying with all her might to return to her native Norway. Finally, she gave up and yielded to the wind, fearing her life was over. But instead of being carried to oblivion, she soon found herself in the warm forests and green fields of England, where she made her home and lived out a life of more warmth and abundance than she could have imagined.

If you give up your own ambitions and allow the will of God to carry you to the destination He chooses for you, you will discover a life better than anything you could ever contrive for yourself. The psalmist put it this way, "Delight yourself also in the LORD, and He shall give you the desires of your heart" (Psalm 37:4). Letting go of your ambition may seem risky, but you have the Bible's assurance that it's the only way to a life beyond amazing. And a tremendous reward will be waiting for you at the end when you hear Christ say, "Well done, good and faithful servant; you were faithful over a few things, I will make you ruler over many things. Enter into the joy of your lord" (Matthew 25:21).

Determine to Commit to the Spirit's Direction

Imagine yourself as a house. God comes in to rebuild that house. At first, perhaps, you can understand what He is doing. He is getting the drains right and stopping the leaks in the roof and so on; you knew that those jobs needed doing, and so you are not surprised. But presently He starts knocking the house about in a way that you have a hard time understanding. What is He up to with these changes?

Quite simply, He is building a far different house from the one you imagined. You thought you were going to be made into a decent little cottage. But He is not content with a cottage. He is building a palace. An edifice worthy of Himself in which to live.[2]

So the question is: What do you want your life to be like? A cottage or a palace? Do you desire the nine virtues of a good and joyful life enough to turn your life over to the Holy Spirit? Or do you want to retain control and risk the works of the flesh inching their way into more of your life and leading you further from all possibility of joy? This is not merely a one-time choice but an ongoing one that faces Christians throughout life. We must exercise constant vigilance over our lives and activities, constant openness to the expanded presence of the Holy Spirit, and constant repentance and recommitment each time we drift away from His direction.

The apostle Paul places this choice starkly before us: "For if you live according to the flesh you will die; but if by the Spirit you put to death the deeds of the body, you will live. For as many as are led by the Spirit of God, these are sons of God" (Romans 8:13–14).

What will your life be like when you are led by the Spirit of God? Will all potholes be filled? All detours straightened? All doors opened? No, being Spirit-led doesn't mean your world suddenly becomes the Garden of Eden. You will still deal with the crabgrass and storm clouds of life, but you will see a huge difference in how you deal with them. With the Holy Spirit at home in your heart, those nine virtues will begin to grow. As you nourish them with God's Word and repair them with repentance, they will mature into a person ready to face each day with confidence and joy.

The fruit of the Spirit is about transformation—making you into something as different from what you were as a butterfly differs from a caterpillar; turning you from a creature that crawls into one that soars. It is by the immeasurable love and grace of God that He offers us His own power to do what we cannot do for ourselves.

Our initial attempts at walking under the control of the Holy Spirit are usually fumbling and ineffective, but He pays us the compliment of taking our attempts seriously and applauding them for the desire they display.

I have a friend whose daughter enrolled in grade-school band. He loved to attend the concerts, and a neighbor asked him why. How could he stand all the missed beats and sour notes? My friend replied, "Well, I guess I just hear what they intend." God hears what we intend. He loves hearing us attempt to play His music, sour notes and all. In fact, He does even better than that. He not only hears what we intend, but by the power of His Holy Spirit, He turns our fumbling efforts into glorious masterpieces.

Don't Quit, Keep Playing

A mother had a young son who was learning to play the piano. His attention often wandered from the keyboard, and she thought it would encourage him to attend a concert of a master pianist. After they were seated, the mother spotted a friend and left her seat to greet her. Her son, always curious, took the opportunity to explore the grand music hall. Soon he wandered through a door marked "No Admittance."

When the house lights dimmed, the mother returned to her seat and discovered that her child was missing. Before she could react, the curtains opened on the spotlighted Steinway at center stage, and the audience erupted with a mix of laughter and anger. When the mother saw the cause of their reaction, she gasped in horror. There at the keyboard sat her little boy, innocently picking out "Twinkle, Twinkle Little Star."

At that moment, the piano master made his entrance. He quickly moved to the piano and whispered in the boy's ear, "Don't quit; keep playing."

Then, the great piano master leaned over the boy and, with his left hand, began filling in a bass accompaniment. A moment later, his right arm reached around to the other side and added a running obbligato. When the last note sounded, the mesmerized audience thundered its applause. Together the old master and the young novice had transformed an awkward moment into a remarkably creative experience.

This is what God does with us. No matter how hard we try to live godly lives, our efforts come up short. But when God enters, He turns our halting music into a masterpiece. This is what Paul was telling us when he wrote, "Work out your own salvation with fear and trembling; for it is God who works in you both to will and to do for His good pleasure" (Philippians 2:12–13). We provide the effort with our desire, our study, and our repentance. But it is God who provides the power by working in us to do His will. The result is a beautiful, transformed life.

The indispensable key, as the great piano master told the little boy, is "Don't quit; keep playing."

APPLICATION

Personal Questions

1. Describe a choice you made that dramatically affected the course of your life.

   a. What happened, and what did you do?

   b. What did you learn, and how did you grow?

2. Write out John Stott's morning prayer. Consider praying this for yourself every morning this week.

3. Why is it important to devote yourself to God's Word?

4. Do you think of "dying to your own ambition" as a good thing or a bad thing? Explain why or why not.

Read Psalm 37:4 and Matthew 25:21. What are the rewards of allowing God to be in charge of your ambitions?

5. Have you fully given control of your life to the Holy Spirit?

  a. In what areas of your life have you done well in engaging with the Holy Spirit?

  b. In what areas can you do better, and how?

6. Describe what an amazing life looks like according to what you have learned in this study.

Group Questions

1. Discuss some of the major decisions people in your group have had to make in their lives.

  a. How did those decisions change you?

  b. How did you grow, and what did you learn from them?

2. Why is it important to be filled with the Holy Spirit when trying to live a life beyond amazing?

3. List the six decisions discussed in this lesson that will help you live a life engaged with the Holy Spirit. Share some practical examples for each.

-
-
-
-
-
-

4. Read Galatians 5:22–23 and discuss the following questions:

   a. What have you learned in this study that will inspire you to live a life beyond amazing?

   b. How can you help each other pursue an amazing life?

5. Review John Stott's daily prayer for an amazing life. Take a few minutes to pray this prayer for each member in the group.

DID YOU KNOW?

Given how the word *fill* is understood today, it would be easy to misunderstand Paul's use of it in Ephesians 5:18: "Be filled with the Spirit." When we fill a swimming pool, we don't fill it *totally* full, nor do we fill a wheelbarrow *completely* full of dirt when gardening. Rather, we fill them *mostly* full. But the Greek word for "be filled" almost always carries the connotation of *completely full*. In fact, it can mean "to finish, to accomplish, to fill amply, to complete"—all words that signify a complete filling. When Paul says to be filled with the Spirit, it doesn't mean mostly filled. If it did, that would allow room for a second "master." And Jesus said we cannot serve more than one (Luke 16:13).

Notes

1. John Stott, quoted in Christopher J. Wright, *Cultivating the Fruit of the Spirit* (Downers Grove, IL: InterVarsity Press, 2017), 1.
2. C. S. Lewis, *Mere Christianity* (New York: Macmillan, 1943, 1945, 1952), 160.

Leader's Guide

Thank you for your commitment to lead a group through *A Life Beyond Amazing*. Being a leader has its own rewards. You may discover that your walk with the Lord deepens through this experience. Throughout the study guide, your group will explore new topics and review study questions that encourage thought-provoking group discussion.

The lessons in this study guide are suitable for Sunday school classes, small-group studies, elective Bible studies, or home Bible study groups. Each lesson is structured to provoke thought and help you grow in your knowledge and understanding of God. There are multiple components in this section that can help you structure your lessons and discussion time, so make sure you read and consider each one.

Before You Begin

Before you begin each meeting, make sure you and your group are well-versed with the content of the lesson. Every person should have his or her own study guide so they can follow along and write in the study guide if need be. When possible, the study guide should be used with the corresponding audio series. You may wish to assign the study guide lesson as homework prior to the meeting of the group and then use the meeting time to listen to the message and discuss the lesson.

To ensure that everyone has a chance to participate in the discussion, the ideal size for a group is around eight to ten people. If there are more than ten people, try to break up the bigger group into smaller subgroups. Make sure the members are committed to participating each week, as this will help create stability and help you better prepare the structure of the meeting.

At the beginning of the study each week, start the session with a question to challenge group members to think about the issues you will be discussing. The members can answer briefly, but the goal is to have an idea in their mind as you go over the lesson. This allows the group members to become engaged and ready to interact with the group.

After reviewing the lesson, try to initiate a free-flowing discussion. Invite group members to bring questions and insights they may have discovered to the next meeting, especially if they were unsure of the meaning of some parts of the lesson. Be prepared to discuss how biblical truth applies to the world we live in today.

Weekly Preparation

As the group leader, here are a few things that you can do to prepare for each meeting:

- *Choose whether or not you will play the audio message during your small-group session.* If you decide to play the message from Dr. Jeremiah as part of the meeting, you will need to adjust the group time accordingly (see the next section for options).

- *Make sure you are familiar with the material in the lesson.* Make sure you understand the content of the lesson so you know how to structure group time and are prepared to lead group discussion.

- *Decide, ahead of time, which questions you want to discuss.* Depending on how much time you have each week, you may not be able to reflect on every question. Select specific questions that you feel will evoke the best discussion.

- *Take prayer requests.* At the end of your discussion, take prayer requests from your group members and pray for each other.

Structuring the Discussion Time

If you need help in organizing your time when planning your group Bible study, here are two schedules, for sixty minutes and ninety minutes, that can give you a structure for the lesson:

Option 1 (Listen to Audio CD)	60 Minutes	90 Minutes
WELCOME: Members arrive and get settled	N/A	5 minutes
GETTING STARTED QUESTION: Prepares the group for interacting with one another	5 minutes	15 minutes
MESSAGE: Listen to the audio CD	40 minutes	40 minutes
DISCUSSION: Discuss group study questions	10 minutes	25 minutes
PRAYER AND APPLICATION : Final application for the week and prayer before dismissal	5 minutes	5 minutes

Option 2 (No Audio CD)	60 Minutes	90 Minutes
WELCOME: Members arrive and get settled	5 minutes	10 minutes
GETTING STARTED QUESTION: Prepares the group for interacting with one another	10 minutes	10 minutes
MESSAGE: Review the lesson	15 minutes	25 minutes
DISCUSSION: Discuss group study questions	25 minutes	35 minutes
PRAYER AND APPLICATION : Final application for the week and prayer before dismissal	5 minutes	10 minutes

As the group leader, it is up to you to keep track of the time and keep things moving along according to your schedule. If your group is having a good discussion, don't feel the need to stop and move on to the next question. Remember, the purpose is to pull together ideas and share unique insights on the lesson. Make time each week to discuss how to apply these truths to living for Christ today. The purpose of discussion is for everyone to participate, but don't be concerned if certain group members are more quiet—they may be internally reflecting on the questions and need time to process their ideas before they can share them.

Group Dynamics

Leading a group study can be a rewarding experience for you and your group members—but that doesn't mean there won't be challenges. Certain members may feel uncomfortable discussing topics that they consider very personal and might be afraid of being called on. Some members might have disagreements on specific issues. To help prevent these scenarios, consider the following ground rules:

- If someone has a question that may seem off topic, suggest that it is discussed at another time, or ask the group if they are okay with addressing that topic.

- If someone asks a question you don't know the answer to, confess that you don't know and move on. If you feel comfortable, invite other group members to give their opinions or share their comments based on personal experience.

- If you feel like a couple of people are talking much more than others, direct questions to people who may not have shared yet. You could even ask the more dominating members to help draw out the quiet ones.

- When there is a disagreement, encourage the group members to process the matter in love. Invite members from opposing sides to evaluate their opinions and consider the ideas of the other members. Lead the group through Scripture that addresses the topic, and look for common ground.

When issues arise, encourage your group to think of Scripture: "Love one another" (John 13:34), "If it is possible, as far as it depends on you, live at peace with everyone" (Romans 12:18 NIV), and "Be quick to listen, slow to speak and slow to become angry" (James 1:19 NIV).

About
Dr. David Jeremiah and Turning Point

D r. David Jeremiah is the founder of Turning Point, a ministry committed to providing Christians with sound Bible teaching relevant to today's changing times through radio and television broadcasts, audio series, books, and live events. Dr. Jeremiah's common-sense teaching on topics such as family, prayer, worship, angels, and biblical prophecy forms the foundation of Turning Point.

David and his wife, Donna, reside in El Cajon, California, where he serves as the senior pastor of Shadow Mountain Community Church. David and Donna have four children and twelve grandchildren.

In 1982, Dr. Jeremiah brought the same solid teaching to San Diego television that he shares weekly with his congregation. Shortly thereafter, Turning Point expanded its ministry to radio. Dr. Jeremiah's inspiring messages can now be heard worldwide on radio, television, and the Internet.

Because Dr. Jeremiah desires to know his listening audience, he travels nationwide holding ministry rallies and spiritual enrichment conferences that touch the hearts and lives of many people. According to Dr. Jeremiah, "At some point in time, everyone reaches a turning point; and for every person, that moment is unique, an experience to hold onto forever. There's so much changing in today's world that sometimes it's difficult to choose the right path. Turning Point offers people an understanding of God's Word as well as the opportunity to make a difference in their lives."

Dr. Jeremiah has authored numerous books, including *Escape the Coming Night* (Revelation), *The Handwriting on the Wall* (Daniel), *Overcoming Loneliness, Prayer—The Great Adventure, God in You* (Holy Spirit), *When Your World Falls Apart, Slaying the Giants in Your Life, My Heart's Desire, Hope for Today, Captured by Grace, Signs of Life, What in the World Is Going On?, The Coming Economic Armageddon, I Never Thought I'd See the Day!, God Loves You: He Always Has—He Always Will, Agents of the Apocalypse, Agents of Babylon, Revealing the Mysteries of Heaven,* and *People Are Asking . . . Is This the End?*

Stay Connected to Dr. David Jeremiah

Take advantage of two great ways to let Dr. David Jeremiah give you spiritual direction every day! Both are absolutely FREE.

Turning Points Magazine and Devotional

Receive Dr. David Jeremiah's magazine, *Turning Points*, each month:

- Thematic study focus
- 48 pages of life-changing reading
- Relevant articles
- Special features
- Daily devotional readings
- Bible study resource offers
- Live event schedule
- Radio & television information

Daily Turning Point E-Devotional

Start your day off right! Find words of inspiration and spiritual motivation waiting for you on your computer every morning! Receive a daily e-devotion communication from David Jeremiah that will strengthen your walk with God and encourage you to live the authentic Christian life.

There are two easy ways to sign up for these free resources from Turning Point. Visit us online at www.DavidJeremiah.org and select "Subscribe to Daily Devotional by Email" or visit the home page and find Daily Devotional to subscribe to your monthly copy of *Turning Points*.